Sergio M. Moccia

The level of protection provided by Chinese labour law compared to German labour law

IGEL Verlag

Sergio M. Moccia

The level of protection provided by Chinese labour law compared to German labour law

1. Auflage 2008 | ISBN: 978-3-86815-045-2

Die Deutsche Bibliothek verzeichnet diesen Titel in der Deutschen Nationalbibliografie. Bibliografische Daten sind unter http://dnb.ddb.de verfügbar.

IGEL Verlag

Table of Contents Page

I. Table of Figures Page

II. List of Abbreviations

FDI	Foreign Direct Investment
BDI	Bundesverband der deutschen Industrie
BDA	Bundesvereinigung der deutschen Arbeitgeber
ACFTU	All-China Federation of Trade Unions
CCP	Chinese Communist Party
FESCO	Foreign Enterprise Service Company
PRC	People's Republic of China
SEZ	Special Economic Zone
GDP	Gross Domestic Product
FIE	Foreign Invested Enterprise
USA	United States of America
RMB	Renminbi
IOC	International Olympic Committee
LSL	Labour Standard Law
ITUC	International Trade Union Cooperation
HR	Human Resource

III. Executive summary

The Thesis "The level of protection provided by Chinese labour law compared to German labour law as a stimuli for western investment in the People's Republic of China" describes the Chinese Labour Law and traces back the sources of the Chinese Labour Law regulations. In the first section, the German Labour Law and some of the most important clauses are explained. In further sections, the Chinese Labour Law itself and its coherent development, the main landmarks and the similarities to the German Labour Law, with its Romanist Tradition, are reflected. In particular the situation of the unions and their influence on management polices are named.

Further more, this thesis displays the current situation in the Chinese corporate world and its relation towards the Chinese Labour Law. With the elaboration of three chosen cases, this thesis highlights the enforcement level and the core aspects of Chinese Labour Law that are frequently violated within Chinese joint-ventures and their partners from abroad, either from Asian or Western developed nations.

In addition, this thesis focuses on the situation in Taiwan and Hong Kong in respect to their Labour Law systems and gives a brief overview over their core aspects and its future perspective and likelihood to keep its sovereignty under the increasing influence of China mainland.

One of the main aspects of this thesis is discussed in the sections dealing with the New Chinese Labour Law of 2007 and its upcoming implementation on the 1st of January 2008. Issues concerning the development and core improvements are evaluated and precisely explained. Further more, the ramifications and main changes that are likely to emerge in the near future will be discussed. This thesis will also shed some light on the reactions of the work force in China and multinationals in general. The fears and hopes that go hand in hand with the implementation of the new draft.

Last but not least, this thesis will give proposals and suggestion to German and Western companies how to deal with labour law related issues that are planning to enter this viable and fast growing market. Moreover, this dissertation will give an overview over the main aspects in terms of Chinese Labour Law regulations that should be considered in order to establish a successful business in the People's Republic of China.

1. Introduction

China's transition from an unproductive rural economy to a manufacturing powerhouse has been referred to as the "Chinese miracle". Growth has skyrocketed, exports have boomed and incomes have improved. For many in China, the transformation of the last 20 years has resulted in rising standards of living along with unprecedented consumer choice. For businesses around the world, this miracle has given them access to new markets and to a cheap and compliant work-force. Indeed China's export success has been led by industries paying unnaturally low wages – from 1985/ 95 to 2002 total accumulative inflows of FDI rose from 11.7 billion Dollars to 52.7 billion Dollars[1].

In China's trade relationships with more advanced East Asian economies, such as Japan, Taiwan, Hong Kong, and Korea, entire industries are relocating to China, typically those which have high labour-input requirements. In addition, China is participating in multi-stage production arrangements with its neighbours, whereby China adds value by providing labour in the assembly of finished machinery and high technology equipment. Its main imports include aircraft, spacecraft, machinery and fertilizer.

But what does Chinese Labour Law have to do with the emergence of the future economic superpower and how important is this fact for China, the Chinese workforce and the investors from Germany and other western societies? There is still a prevalent opinion among western societies that Labour Law is non-existent in the People's Republic of China. Certainly, pessimists would agree. But there is a Chinese Labour Law Code, and in fact, it is strongly comparable to those of western societies. In particular, the German Labour Law Code functioned as a basis for the Chinese Labour Law regulations and has thus had a great influence until today.

In addition, the new draft of 2007 and its implementation in January 2008 has attracted worldwide interest and triggered a lot of controversial opinions. The Chinese Labour Law Code is gaining significantly in importance and especially overseas co-operations have to reconsider their operations policies in China. We have to be

1 http://www.tdctrade.com/econforum/boc/boc030101.htm; See Arbeitsrecht07.pdf; p. 7

aware of the fact, that foreign direct invested companies and their Chinese partners accounted for 65 % of all measured exports in 2003 and the figure has been growing ever since[2]. This is the reason why German companies and their western competitors in particular have to face current legal developments and might have to start switching their mind-set, concerning their employment policies in China.

This thesis will highlight the landmarks of the Chinese Labour Law development, from the early beginnings until the present day. It will display a sharp overview over the German Labour Law which functioned as a role model for the Chinese Labour Law in several occasions. By discussing some selected cases, this thesis will display the most frequently violated labour laws and give suggestions how companies from Germany and other key source countries of FDI should conduct their business in China and its viable and fast growing economy.

---

2 http://www.laborstrategies.blogs.com/global_labor_strategies/files/behind_the_great_wall_of_china.pdf ; See Arbeitsrecht21.pdf; p. 7

2. The German Labour Law

This section will deal with the German Labour Law in order to give an overview over the most important aspects of this labour code. Many of the regulations given below formed the basis for the development of the Chinese Labour Code. The Chinese Labour Law is substantially influenced by the Civil Law system and derives from countries with a Romanist tradition, Germany in particular[3].

2.1 The Contract of employment

As a rule, the contract of employment is concluded for an unlimited period[4]. The employer and the employee are allowed to clinch a contract for a limited time period.

The duration of fixed-term contracts must be set according to objective conditions such as a specific termination date, the completion of a specific task, or the occurrence of a specific incident[5]. In general, it also has to be based on the justifications which comprise motives such as the temporary requirement of a certain type of work, a limitation in order to make the worker's access into professional life easier or the replacement of a sick employee.

2.1.1 Probation

When concluding a labour contract the parties often agree upon a probationary period of up to 6 months. During this period, the employee can be dismissed with a two weeks notice[6]. Alternatively, the parties may enter the employment relationship by agreeing on a contract that is limited up to 6 months.[7].

---

3 http://www.nyulawglobal.org/globalex/China.htm; See Arbeitsrecht01.pdf; page 1
4 cp. German Civil Code; sec. 620 para 2
5 See Wörlen Kokemoor; Arbeitsrecht; p. 43
6 cp. German Civil Code, sec. 622 para. 3
7 http://www.info-arbeitsrecht.de/Kuendigungsschutz/kuendigungsschutz.html; See Arbeitsrecht02.pdf

2.1.2 Termination of employment

The major sources of regulation in this matter are the Civil Code and the Protection against Dismissals Act. However, the latter applies only to establishments regularly employing more than five full-time employees.

Also, a worker must have completed a qualifying period of six months work without interruption to be eligible for protection under this law[8].

German labour law makes a distinction between ordinary termination (with notice), whereby the employment relationship is ended when the period of notice expires, and extraordinary termination (without notice).In the latter type of termination, the notification effects the immediate cancellation of the employment relationship[9].

In both cases, termination at the initiative of the employer is limited by law. Periods of notice are stipulated by the law. The minimum statutory period is four weeks, and it is increased by one month each time the worker has completed the following working periods for one and the same company.

Figure 1: Working time period and cancellation period

Working time or period	cancellation period
Two years	one month
Five years	two months
Eight years	three months
Ten years	four months
Twelve years	five months
Fifteen years	six months
Twenty years	seven months

However, years of service before the employee has reached the age of 25 years are not taken into consideration to calculate his/her entitlement to notice[10]. Collective agreements may specify longer or

8 See Rüdiger Krause; Arbeitsrecht I; Individualarbeitsrecht; P. 299

9 cp. German Civil Code; sec. 622 & sec.626

10 cp. German Civil Code; sec 622 para. 2

shorter periods of notice, whereas individual contracts of employment may only specify longer periods of notice[11]. As of May 1, 2000, notice must be given in writing in order to be legally binding[12].

2.1.3 Extraordinary dismissal

There are certain cases in which it is actually possible to terminate an employment relationship prior to the end of the notice or the end before the work contract expires. This is the case, if it is unacceptable, in good faith, for the company to employ the employee any longer as it is the case with serious misconduct. When ever the employer notices a serious misconduct, the employer has to react within two weeks[13].

In case of existence of a work council, the employer is obliged to consult it during a dismissal procedure, even though the council's response is not binding for the employer. The works council has a period of three days, in case of summary dismissal and one week in case of ordinary termination to agree or declare reservations in writing; otherwise an agreement is presumed by law. The termination of a contract without proper hearing of the works council is ineffective[14].

Special rules apply to mass lay-offs in establishments employing more than twenty employees, which call for the consultation of the works council and the drawing of a social plan. Some groups of employees benefit from particular protection against ordinary and extraordinary dismissal due to certain individual circumstances including disabled workers, pregnant women and work council members[15].

A worker who intends to fight his/her termination must file a submission before a labour court within a time limit of three weeks

---

11 cp. German Civil Code; sec 622 para. 4

12 http://www.info-arbeitsrecht.de/Kuendigungsschutz/kuendigungsschutz.html; See Arbeitsrecht02.pdf

13 See Wilfried Berkowski; Die Personen- und verhaltensbedingte Kündigung; p. 266/267

14 See Kittner & Zwanziger; Arbeitsrecht; p. 1522

15 ibid; p. 1536/1537

as of the date he/she has received his/her notice. If the court is not convinced that either the ordinary termination is socially justified, or the extraordinary dismissal is for important reasons, it may order the worker's reinstatement, with back pay, unless it feels that such a measure is impractical, in which case it may order the employer to pay compensation, normally equal to one month pay per each month of service, with a maximum of twelve months, or eighteen months if the worker is more than 55 years old and has twenty or more years of service[16].

2.2 Trade union and employers' association regulation

Freedom of association of both workers and employers is guaranteed as a basic right under the Basic Law. This includes the right of individuals to form associations, to join an existing association, to participate actively in an association, to leave an association or to not belong to any association. It also contains the association's protection against any influence of the state or any attack of an individual[17].

An association within the meaning of the Basic Law is a voluntary permanent joining together, which must not be limited to one company. Additionally, any association must consider itself as a representative of either the employees or the employers and must explicitly work towards the conclusion of collective agreements.

2.2.1 Trade unions

There is no trade union law in Germany. Even though trade unions are generally defined as associations with no legal capacity, they are legally entitled to collectively bargain as well as to take legal action or to be taken to court[18]. The duties and rights of trade union members are laid down in the relevant trade union's constitution. Even though the constitutions may vary between different trade unions, they traditionally establish similar essential duties and rights. Members are obliged to pay union dues, of which the amount is based on the individual wage level. At the same time,

---

16 ibid; p. 1553

17 cp. German Basic Law; Art. 9

18 cp. Act on Collective Agreements; sec. 2 para. 1

they are entitled to support in labour disputes as well as to receive legal advice[19].

2.2.2 Employers' associations

Employers' associations are generally defined as associations with legal capacity.

Many of the regional associations are industry-based and the same branch is finally merged in an association at federal level. The federal associations of the different branches are unified in the two most important central confederations, the Federal Union of German Industry (BDI)[20] and the Confederation of German Employers' Associations (BDA)[21]. The BDA represents the enterprises' interest as an employer, whereas the BDI seeks to further their economic and political interests. However they are increasingly working together and try to benefit form their synergies. This progress peeked into the establishment of a common steering committee[22].

2.3 Collective Bargaining and Agreements

Collective bargaining is regulated by the Act on Collective Agreements, which, however, does not mandate a given structure of collective bargaining. The legal capacity to collectively bargain is possessed by the trade unions on the one hand and the employer's associations as well as the individual employer on the other[23].

In fact, collective bargaining mostly takes place at the branch level, even though, in some cases, trade unions may also bargain with the individual employer, provided that it is permitted by their constitutions. A prohibition of the employer's organization against individual collective bargaining of its members does not affect the

19 http://www.dgb.de/mitglied_werden/index_html; See Arbeitsrecht06.pdf

20 http://www.bdi.eu/de/bdi/72.htm; See Arbeitsrecht03.pdf

21 http://www.bda-online.de/www/bdaonline.nsf/id/AufgabenundZiele; See Arbeitsrecht04.pdf

22 http://www.manager-magazin.de/koepfe/artikel/0,2828,446123,00.html; See Arbeitsrecht05.pdf

23 cp. Act on Collective Agreements; sec. 2 para. 1

validity of the collective agreement but results in the employer's duty to pay damages[24].

Collective agreements have three characterizing functions:

- the protective function which manifest itself in setting minimum labour standards;
- the rationalizing function that puts working life in order and alignment;
- and the peacekeeping function, in other words, that as long as the collective agreement remains in force new demands and labour disputes about included topics are absolutely banned (industrial peace).

Any collective agreement is a contract, which entails two parts. The first part, part under the law of contracts, deals with rights and duties of the contractual partners. The two main obligations of the partners are industrial peace and the duty to use all possible means to make sure that their members stick to the agreement. The second part of the collective agreement sets rules related to labour contracts, to operational questions and to the works constitution within the meaning of the Works Constitution Act. This distinction is important for the collective agreement's period of validity[25]. Generally, a collective agreement ends when the period of time expires for which the agreement was concluded. It may be terminated earlier at one party's legal initiative or by mutual agreement. In any case, the part under the law of contract necessarily ends at the same time[26]. Unlike this, the legal norms setting part stays in force until it is replaced by either an individual contractual agreement or a works agreement or in particular by legal norms of a new collective agreement[27]. What personal validity is concerned, a collective agreement is generally binding for those who are members of the relevant trade union and employers' association at the time when the collective agreement came into effect. Its rules are hence applicable to the individual employment relationship. However, the employer's commitment is sufficient for

---

24 See Wörlen & Kokemoor; Arbeitsrecht; p. 201

25 ibid; p. 203/ 204

26 ibid; p. 208

27 cp. Act on Collective agreements; sec.1 para.1 & sec. 4 para. 5

the application of legal norms related to operational questions or to the works constitution[28].

[28] cp. Act on Collective agreements; sec.3 para.1 & sec. 3 para. 2

3. The Development of the Chinese Labour Law

This section will focus on the Contract Employment System and its implementation in 1995. It is interesting to see how similar the content of the German Labour Code actually is, compared to Chinese one. Later sections will highlight this matter of fact.

However, the creation of a Labour Law Code in China has been a rocky road that went through more than 40 drafts until it came into effect. One of the major supporters of the reformation of the Chinese Labour Law was the ACFTU, the umbrella organization of all unions in China[29]. This state-directed organization has extremely lobbied the central government and has insisted on initiating the Chinese Labour Law from 1994[30].

Further more, the emergence of the particular term "socialist market economy" (Chinese term: shehui zhuyi shichang jingji) which became part of the official lexicon in 1992, at the 14th congress of the Chinese Communist Party (CCP) led to the adoption of a new approach to economic development that triggered changes in the legal system, including the field of labour and employment law. Perhaps the most significant development was in the realm of labour mobility, both for rural and urban populations. Peasants were permitted to seek employment outside of agriculture, beyond the confines of their villages. Urban residents were no longer assigned to jobs in a system of bureaucratic allocation, and thereafter, prevented, by the legal and economic disincentives, from seeking alternative job opportunities.[31]

3.1 The Contract employment system and its position in the Labour Code

The successive chapter will elaborate on the most significant labour-related aspects of the economic reforms in the People's Republic of China. In 1980, first actions were undertaken, as a central government initiative. Further down the road, the geographic scope of the actions was amplified; from local to national regulation. This development took place in 1986. Until recently, in 1994, the contract

29 http://www.weltderarbeit.de/bericht2.htm; See Arbeitsrecht25.pdf

30 See Der chinesische Arbeitsmarkt,; Jutta Hebel Anita Chan; p. 252

31 cp. Labour Law in China; Hillary K. Josephs; p. 1/2

employment system became part of China's first labour code. The so-called Labour Law Act represents the most important legal source in this field.

The other actor besides the ACFTU that pushed the establishment of the contract Employment system was the Chinese government itself whose main concern has been to promote economic development and greater participation in the global economy. The introduction of a "socialist market economy" should be the backbone of this development. Its key objective was to foster productivity in the agricultural and industrial sectors[32].

In the past, Labour allocation was undertaken by administrative assignment, until reforms in the early 1980s became finally effective. Sources indicate that the so-called "unified placement system" (Chinese term: tong'yi fenpei) controlled more than 50 per cent of the hiring of workers and staff. The Ministry of Labour and its local bureaus were responsible for the allocation of workers. "Unified placement" was mainly applied to graduates of higher education. It prevailed until the mid-1990s.

One major downside of the administrative allocation of labour was its practical lack to guarantee employment for all job-seekers. In the early 1980s, guaranteed work for all was not doable under the inherent circumstances.

By implementing the dual planned-market approach in the agricultural sector, it also undertook reform of the urban industrial economy, particularly state enterprises in order to create a more viable environment.

State enterprises were responsible for a large share of industrial output. Quadrupling annual industrial and agricultural output value by the end of the twentieth century was the core objective of the Central Government. The share of industrial output by state enterprises plummeted from 77.6 percent in the late 1980s to 25.5 percent at the present day[33]

According to figures from the year 2002, state-owned enterprises account for 27 percent of the Gross Industrial Output Value, and equals 300 Billion Euros. Although most of the state-owned

32 cp. Labour Law in China; Hillary K. Josephs; p. 12/13

33 cp. Labour Law in China; Hillary K. Josephs; p. 14/15

enterprises remain in operation only because of governmental subsidies (the number of companies has declined to 67119 in 2002 compared to 76412 in 2001)[34] , their output still accounts for a significant proportion of total production.

By allowing workers to switch jobs, the contract employment system would promote diffusion of technical knowledge, reduce overspecialization, and respond to changes in individual attitudes towards work. [35]

3.2 Difficulties and scant attempts to alleviate the situation

Talking about labour-reforms and the draft of the contract employment system in 1994, it is essential to shed some light on the situation of China in terms of its economic situation, the power of state-owned enterprises and prevalent customs that were and are even today widely accepted among the Chinese work force.

3.2.1 Reward based on status rather than performance

Historically the labour force of state enterprises was subdivided into two basic groups, the permanent work force and the temporary workforce. By starting the employment the status was fixed. Only a minority of highly skilled employees were able to access permanent status.

Permanent status allowed such workers to benefit from the full range of fringe benefits provided by the employer, including subsidized medical care, housing, and educational facilities. Such workers enjoyed immunity from dismissal. Only in cases of outrageous misconduct such as chronic absenteeism or criminal conviction (corruption) could lead to a dismissal. Even in case of bankruptcy; permanent workers were normally relocated to other permanent job locations.[36].

---

34 http://www.chinapolitik.de/studien/china_analysis/no_45.pdf ; See Arbeitsrecht09.pdf; p. 21

35 cp. Labour Law in China; Hillary K. Josephs; p. 16

36 cp. Labour Law in China; Hillary K. Josephs; p. 17

Temporary workers did not capitalize on the benefits mentioned above. In the 1980s, state enterprises were allowed to hire great amounts of temporary workers from rural areas. Management preferred temporarily migrant workers more because they were willing to endure hardship and showed more commitment for their tasks. Managements of state-owned enterprises would have hired more of them, if there were no restrictions on hiring and coherent administrative costs. However, in many cases, temporary workers were hired simply because no one else was willing to do the work. At that juncture, the official opinion was that temporary workers and permanent workers were not suitable for one another and occupy different strata in the occupational hierarchy of the firm[37].

3.2.2 Skills did not meet the job requirements

In the late 1950s, government labour and education bureaus filled vacancies in state owned enterprises through a system of administrative assignment. As already mentioned, the so-called "unified placement system" was responsible for the allocation of the job-seekers. The whole process was never questioned. As a practical matter, both, the employer and the employee could not refuse the job allocation.

The individual's interest, aptitude, or training, was not taken into consideration during the job allocation process. Once assigned for a job, a worker was not allowed to quit and look for another position. The enterprises had no possibility to dismiss a worker on the ground that the worker was "unsuitable" for the job[38]. In other words, job positions requiring skilled workers could be filled by unskilled or not suitable employees.

But not only had the administrative assignment adverse knock-on effects, state enterprises had to cope with difficulties arising from the so-called "substitution system" (Chinese term: dingti zhidu). Under this system, a retiree from a permanent job in a state owned enterprise could designate one of his children to succeed him as a permanent employee in the same enterprise, although not necessarily in the same position as held by the parent.

---

37 ibid; p. 19/20

38 ibid; p. 20/ 21

This right was widely accepted by the Chinese population beginning starting in the early 1950s. Enterprises did benefit from this habitude in certain occasions. Companies could reduce their efforts to recruit new working staff. Moreover, because of the personal ties between the potential worker and the future retiree, the designated successor felt obligated to perform well in the job[39].

The first steps to encounter this situation were undertaken in 1986. Advertisements of positions in state owned enterprises were initiated, mandating examination of prospective hires. By doing so, the State Councils were hoping to allocate more qualified and skilled workers for the appropriate positions. But until the present day; the "substitution system" could not be abolished completely. There are still many regions that abide by this system[40].

3.2.3 Disequilibrium of Labour and Supply

Chinese labour force could be characterized during the 1970s by an oversupply of unskilled labour and an undersupply of skilled workers and professional manpower. To face this development, a score of strategies were amended to encounter this issue.

For instance state enterprises were overstaffed, forcing of the substitution system, the expansion of employment in the light industries and services, and the removal of the ban on self-employment were the most significant steps[41].

3.3 The Way to the Contract Employment System

First steps ever reported were already undertaken in 1979, when the Sino Foreign Joint Venture Law was introduced in order to promulgate new ways of labour recruitment and remuneration. This was the basis for a multitude of national and local labour law regulations[42].

In this Section we will limit the amount of landmarks by focusing on three major sources of the contract employment system:

---

39 ibid; p. 22

40 cp. Labour Law in China; Hillary K. Josephs; p. 24

41 ibid; p. 25

42 See Der chinesische Arbeitsmarkt ; Jude Howell; p. 138

(1) The 1983 Notice of the Ministry of Labour and Personnel on Active Trial Implementation of the Contract Employment System

(2) The 1986 State Council Provisional Regulations on the implementation of the Contract Employment System in State Owned Enterprises, as amended in 1992;

(3) The Labour Law of 1994, promulgated by the Standing Committee of the National People's Congress

For a long period of time, the policy goals and implementing mechanisms of the law did not markedly change. During its evolution, the language of the law was transformed from hortatory to mandatory, from general to specific[43]. This is the usual terminology of law implementation in China.

3.3.1 The Ministry Notice

The Ministry Notice was one of the major landmarks that contributed to the final draft of the Chinese Contract Employment system. In this Notice, some basic aspects of German Labour Law were adopted and submitted in 1980. It did not provide sanctions for non-compliance; it was more a political statement which underpinned more general aims, rather than an administrative regulation.

The Ministry Notice targeted some main aspects of today's contract employment system. It focussed on misbehaviours in state owned enterprises. There, the vast majority of workers enjoyed life tenure. Individual achievements should be closely tied to remuneration and thus to higher wages. The main objective was to create an environment that could promote a commitment to higher output. A further goal was to create a situation of greater autonomy to form employment relationships for both, the employer and the employee. As the Ministry Notice stated, contract workers must be selected on the basis of individual performance and the employment relationship must be founded on "equality and mutual benefit"[44].

---

43 cp. Labour Law in China; Hillary K. Josephs; p. 26

44 ibid; p. 30

The Ministry Notice set forth a score of basic aspects to encounter customary behaviours[45]:

- an employment relationship comes into effect through a formal written agreement
- each party is allowed to terminate the contract with less difficulties
- labour disputes should be resolved by a formal system of third party resolution

The Ministry Notice emphasized the existence of a written contract. However, subsequent experience showed that the writing was constantly disregarded. Although the vast majority of employees did not have an employment contract, labour arbitration panels already took place if there was an "employment relationship in fact". This catalogue of essential terms was carried out in the 1986 regulations and the draft of 1994.[46]

3.3.2 The Contract Employment Regulations

On July 12, 1986, the State Council established these provisional regulations[47]:

(1) Provisional Regulations on the Implementation of the Contract Employment System in State Enterprises

(2) Provisional Regulations on the Hiring of Workers in State Enterprises

(3) Provisional Regulations on the Dismissal of Workers and Staff for Work Violations in State Enterprises

(4) Provisional Regulations on Unemployment Insurance for Workers and Staff Enterprises

(5) Provisional Regulations on the Resolution of Labour Disputes in State Enterprises

---

45 ibid; p. 31

46 cp. Labour Law in China; Hillary K. Josephs; p. 33/34

47 ibid; p. 35

The Contract Employment Regulations stated that every labour contract must cover production or work responsibilities, the period of apprenticeship, the term of contract, working conditions, compensation, labour insurance and fringe benefits, labour discipline, liability for breach, essential terms of the employment contract. These regulations were completely in accordance with the Ministry Notice which preceded them and the Contract Employment System which followed[48].

Four situations being postulated by the Contract Employment Regulations permitted the enterprise to terminate a contract relationship:[49]

(1) If the worker proved being unsatisfactory during the apprenticeship period

(2) If the worker exhausted his official sick leave for nonworking related illness or injury, and still was unable to return to work.

(3) If the worker was dismissed for cause pursuant to the Dismissal Regulations

(4) If the enterprise had been officially notified of impending bankruptcy or had been declared bankrupt

There were also a score of circumstances that expressly prohibited the termination of the contract relationship[50]:

(1) Where the contract term had not yet been expired, unless specific grounds for termination existed

(2) Where the worker had been certified as suffering from a work-related illness or injury

(3) Where the worker was on official sick leave for non-work related illness or injury

(4) Where a female worker was pregnant, on maternity leave, or nursing a child

---

48 ibid; p. 35

49 ibid; p. 36

50 cp. Labour Law in China; Hillary K. Josephs; p. 37

A worker was also allowed to terminate the contract prior to expiration without liability for damages only for specified reasons. These reasons included[51]:

(1) Where working conditions had been officially certified as unsafe or unhealthy

(2) Where the enterprise was unable to pay wages as specified in the contract

(3) Where the worker undertook higher education with the enterprise's approval

(4) Where the enterprise failed to carry out the terms of the contract

(5) Where the enterprise had violated law or policy and had violated the worker's rights

A worker was also allowed to terminate the contract if an enterprise in another jurisdiction demanded for his or her specific skill and qualifications and the local labour bureau where he was currently employed approved of the worker's act of termination. Job-switching was not sanctioned in order to improve one's income or better utilize one's endowments and skills, despite numerous national policy statements urging the exercise of personal initiative and emphasizing the importance of maximizing individual ability[52].

In case of termination of the contract, a month's advance notice was required. In the event of breach, the aggrieved party could maintain a cause of action for damages. If the enterprise terminated the contract, it was obliged to "solicit the opinion" of the trade union and report its action to its department-in charge and the local bureau were not required to "approve" contract termination, in practice, they often exerted pressure on enterprises to retract dismissal decisions.

Many of the discussed aspects in these sections were completely transferred to the Labour Law draft of 1994 and are similar to many

---

51 ibid; p. 37

52 cp. Labour Law in China; Hillary K. Josephs; p. 38

regulations governed by the German Law System and formed the major fundaments of the Contract Employment system.

3.4 The Chinese Labour Law from 1994

So far, this thesis has elaborated on the sources of the Chinese Labour Law and its final expression in the draft of 1994 and its implementation on the July 1, 1995. In the following chapters we will specify the content of the Contract Employment system and highlight some of the regulations that are closely related to the German Labour Law.

3.4.1 Legal Bases

In 1995 labour law was introduced in China[53]. This set of laws is more important than any other regulations provided by several administrative boards, e.g. the Ministry of Labour, the provinces, the autonomous regions and the municipalities. The terms cited by the labor law are not very exact and display a lack of accuracy. This is the reason why local regulations need to be considered. As long as the local regulations do not oppose the terms being described and mentioned in the labor law, companies underlie the set of rules imposed by the autonomous region or city.

The labor law specifications in the diverse areas and autonomous regions, including the municipalities are commonly quite different through out the country. We will take a closer look at the situation, taking two of the most important economic regions of China as an example, entailing the municipalities of Shanghai and Shenzhen and the capital itself, Beijing. The Chinese Labour Law allows municipalities to choose regional solutions to introduce labour law regulations[54]. Shanghai, for instance, launched its own contract employment regulative body in 2002[55]. Some parts of the following section will deal with these regulations.

---

53 cp. Labour Law of the PRC (NPC 05.07.1994)

54 ibid; Art. 106

55 See Arbeit in China; Rolf Geffken; p. 75

3.4.2 Foreign employees

Most of the labour laws affect local Chinese workers and do not affect the overseas employees. For instance, in Shanghai the clinching of a contract of employment, the layoff, the compensation or payment and the social insurance of overseas employees in foreign invested enterprises can be released and regulated by the directorate and freely stipulated within the employment contract[56].

The labour contract between a foreign employee and a local Chinese company can be governed by overseas law[57]. But some details and aspects of the working relation are also mandatory for overseas employees as for instance Chinese regulations on working time, recovering, vacation and anniversary days as well as the work safety terms that are also compulsory for non-locals[58].

Labour law disputes between a foreign employee and his or her Chinese employer need to be discussed by the local Labour Arbitration Commission. The decision by another arbitration court would be ineffective[59].

3.4.3 Representative office

An overseas company can basically employ no Chinese workers within the Chinese borders. But a foreign company is allowed to employ locals in their representative offices. Representative offices do not have the right to employ native workers. There is the possibility to receive employees or workers from the local Foreign Enterprise Service Company (FESCO)[60].

3.4.4 The justification of a working relation

Contract of employment: When a working relation is established an employment contract has to be clinched[61].

---

56 cp. Das Recht der Investitionen in China; Andreas Diem; p. 143
57 cp. Contract Law of the PRC, Art. 126
58 cp. Das Recht der Investitionen in China; Andreas Diem; p. 144
59 Ibid; p. 144
60 cp. Das Recht der Investitionen in China; Andreas Diem; p. 144
61 cp. Labour Law of the PRC; Art. 16 para 2

The contract parties: The participating parties are the foreign directed enterprise and the employee. Considering the set of rules or the law, only persons can be hired that have their registered residence within the same city of the foreign invested enterprise[62]. In reality, however, employees are also employed when they do not have their registered residence in the same town.

Employment prohibitions: It is not allowed to employ certain persons such as minors under sixteen[63], pupils[64] and persons that are still employed with another company. The infringement can lead to compensation[65].

Content of the working contract: The contract of employment has to entail regulations about the duration of the working relation, the type of function, the working safety and working conditions, the payment, the working discipline, the lay off modalities and the accountability in case of contract infringement[66].

Illegality: Individual contracts of employment, which oppose valid laws, are nullified. The nullification has to be approved by an arbitrator commission for labour disputes. The nullification dates then back until the point of conclusion of the contract[67]. In case of disbelief, the nullification only affects the illicit part of the contract.

Formal regulations: Contracts of employment have to be composed in Chinese[68]. In some regions there are regulations that prescribe that contracts of employment need to be declared by the local labour administration or at least approved by this institution. In case of non-abidance the contract of employment can be nullified or rejected[69].

Taking the municipality of Shanghai, the process being described is not compulsory. The contract of employment becomes valid as soon as both attending parties set their sign on the contract. However, the

---

62 cp. Das Recht der Investitionen in China; Andreas Diem; p. 144

63 cp. Labour Law of the PRC; Art. 15

64 cp. Das Recht der Investitionen in China; Andreas Diem; p. 144

65 cp. Labour Law of the PRC; Art. 99

66 ibid; Art. 19

67 ibid; Art. 18 para 2

68 cp. Labour Law of the PRC; Art. 19

69 cp. Das Recht der Investitionen in China; Andreas Diem; p. 145

main clauses and the content of the contract have to be transmitted to the labour office[70].

Compensation modalities: Employees have the possibility to sue their employers for compensation, if the nullification of the contract of employment has to be represented by the employer[71].

3.4.5 Duration of the working relation

A contract of employment can be disposed temporary, indefinite or for the duration of a certain project[72]. But there is a remarkable impediment: If an employee is working for one and the same employer over ten years in a row and both parties would like to continue the working relation, the employee is allowed to ask for an unlimited contract of employment[73].

Also in case of a transmission to the Chinese partner of the joint-venture, the working period being fulfilled by the employee for the overseas company is still valid[74]. But there are municipalities that have changed this rule, e.g. in March 19, 1998 Shanghai introduced a law that impedes the adding of the period being absolved by the foreign employee[75].

Probation: There are some local administrations that have set regulations governing the probation period. This period depends on the duration noted in the contract of employment.

Taking Shanghai as an example, the following respites have been ratified[76]:

Figure 2: Duration of contracts and probation

Duration of contract of employment	admissible probation
Under six months	none
Six to fewer than twelve months	one month
One to fewer than three years	three months
Three years or more	six months

70 ibid; p. 145
71 cp. Labour Law of the PRC; Art.97
72 ibid; Art. 20
73 ibid; Art. 20
74 cp. Das Recht der Investitionen in China; Andreas Diem; p. 146
75 cp. Das Recht der Investitionen in China; Andreas Diem; p. 146
76 cp. Das Recht der Investitionen in China; Andreas Diem; p. 146

Next to the expiration of a short-term contract of employment and the termination of a contract by mutual agreement, it is also possible to end the contract by an instant dismissal or a statutory notice of termination[77].

3.4.6 Dismissal by the employer

The Chinese labour law does not distinguish between worker and appointee. This implies that there are no different cancellation periods. The employer is allowed to cease a working relation by personal individually conditioned reasons[78], by business-related reasons or by the omission of the inherent basis of contract.

Individual-related dismissal without contractual notice of dismissal

An instant dismissal because of person-related reasons is effective in the following situations[79]:

- If the employee does not meet the employers expectation being expressed in the contract
- Whether the employee does markedly violate the framework of rules at his or her working place
- When the employee notably violates his duties or displays corrupt behaviour that encounters the interests of his employer
- In case the employee is facing a prosecution

Individual-related contractual notice of dismissal

The employer is allowed to dismiss his employee within a period of 30 days in the subsequent cases[80]:

- The employee gets ill because of non-business-related issues. If the illness sources back to an activity being exercised during

---

77 cp. Labour Law of the PRC; Art. 24

78 cp. Das Recht der Investitionen in China; Andreas Diem; p. 147

79 cp. Labour Law of the PRC; Art. 25

80 ibid; Art. 26

the leisure time and an appropriate treatment of the injuries does not set back the employee to its previous physical condition and the employee is still qualified to get remedially vacation, then the dismissal is legally provable after the expiration of this certain time period.

- The employee is unable to exercise his function. If the situation does not improve after a course of instruction or a transfer to another working place, the dismissal is valid.

Business-related dismissal

In addition to the quoted reasons of individual-related dismissals, the employee has the possibility to reduce his workforce, when a certain amount is perceived to be redundant. This implies the requirement that the enterprise is running danger to fail and has probably to declare bankruptcy in the near future[81]. Furthermore, if the manufacturer is facing tremendous production inefficiencies or other business-related difficulties, then he is allowed to take actions.

The employer has to treat the employees in a preferential manner that has been dismissed because of the recently described reasons. But only when the employer is capable to expand it's working staff within the next six month after the crisis. This leads to the fact, that a dismissed employer does not receive his full right of freedom of contract rights after the dismissal.

Hearing Rights: The Labour Law desires, that the Union or the workforce have to get filled in and are designated to get a hearing. Further more the local labour administration needs to get notified as well[82].

But it is not mandatory that the Union, workforce or labour administration approves the dismissal. If the information and hearing right is violated by the employer, than the employee has the right or option to sue his former employer for compensation payments[83].

[81] ibid; Art. 27

[82] ibid; Art. 27

[83] cp. Labour Law of the PRC; Art. 98

Omission of the foundation of a contract

The employer has the authorization to dismiss an employee, when the "objective circumstance" that was preventative after the clinching of the contract, have been altered in such a manner that the respective parties, including the employer and the employee are not capable to sustain the working relation The dismissal turns valid as soon as both parties can not agree on the arrangement of new clauses governing the contract of employment[84].

Dismissal Prohibitions

A statutory notice of dismissal can be neglected in case of particular harshness. Reasons for such a rigid behaviour can be the postulation of a dismissal when the employee is currently suffering from a business-related illness or work accident, or if the appointed person is on therapy at that certain juncture. A further reason for the non-allowance of a dismissal is valid, when a woman is about to get a child or is currently pregnant[85].

An employee, who suffers form a business-related illness, "should" resign if his or her illness and the subsequent incapability of working have been classified one to four on a scale from one to ten[86].

3.4.7 Resignation by the employee

The Contract Employment offers also Chinese employees to terminate their contracts of employment under their initiative. The subsequent regulations govern this aspect and show once again, the similarities to the Civil Law System and the German Labour Code.

Dismissal without notice

The employee or worker has the right to resign without notice during his probation period. A further reason can emerge in case the employer threatens the employee or applies violence in order to

---

84 ibid; Art. 26

85 ibid; Art. 29

86 cp. Das Recht der Investitionen in China; Andreas Diem; p. 149

force the respective person to work. Also, whenever the employer is not willing to pay the concerted loan or abide by the agreed terms in the contract[87]. There is no minor bagatelle; the Chinese law enables the employee to resign instantly in case of a minor infringement by the employer. Normally, the courts expect a certain level of contract breach from part of the employer.

Contractual notice of dismissal

A contractual notice of dismissal is always permitted to be expressed throughout the employee. The employee has to hand in the note within 30 days and in written form[88].

3.4.8 Compensation

The payment of compensation during the cancellation of the contract of employment is only rudimentary regulated in the Chinese Labour Law[89]. Most of the provinces, autonomous regions and municipalities have decreed local regulations governing this point[90]. Normally, the employer has to pay compensation in case of a contractual notice of dismissal. Only in case of a legitimate dismissal without notice is the employer released from any receivables on the site of the employee or worker[91]. Therefore, the employer needs to pay compensation when the employee hast do be dismissed because of incapability.

Amount: The extent of compensation depends on the years of service in a company. Usually it is a month salary for each year attended[92]. There are Provinces, in which former contractual relations have to be taken into consideration. In other, if the dismissed employee has had a contract of employment already in the past for the same company, then the level or amount of

87 cp. Labour Law of the PRC; Art. 32
88 ibid; Art. 31
89 ibid; Art. 28
90 cp. Das Recht der Investitionen in China; Andreas Diem; p. 150
91 cp. Labour Law of the PRC; Art. 28
92 cp. Das Recht der Investitionen in China; Andreas Diem; p. 150

compensation raises[93]. But in many Chinese regions, there is a limit for compensation, its maximum or ceiling is set at twelve months[94].

Shanghai: Due to the regulations of the municipality of Shanghai, there is a difference between a unique subsistence payment and a unique illness cost benefit. For the following cases, a unique subsistence payment is intended:

(1) By the termination of a contract in case of enterprise closure[95]

(2) By cancelling the working relation in an amicable environment[96]

(3) By abrogation through the employee, when the employer neglects to pay the loan or salary or other warranted benefits[97]. Further more, if the employer applies violence, threatens the employee or shows illicit constraint of personal freedom in order to force the employee to exercise his or her work[98].

(4) By handing in a statutory notice of termination through the employer because of the following reasons:

   i. Incapability of the employee, to exercise his or her former job or other designated tasks after expiration of the therapy period. The incapability needs to be traced back to an accident during the leisure time[99].

   ii. Incapability of the employee, to exercise his tasks in accordance with usual standard within the company, even after having attended schooling or educational training[100]

   iii. By impossibility of accomplishment of the contract of employment because of changing objective circumstances, in case that the parties are not capable to agree on an adaptation of new contractual terms[101].

---

93 cp. Regulations on the administration of Labour Contracts; Art. 14

94 cp. RSMLP; Art. 18

95 ibid; Art. 14 para 2

96 cp. Labour Law of the PRC; Art 24/28

97 cp. Das Recht der Investitionen in China; Andreas Diem; p. 151

98 ibid; 151

99 ibid; 151

100 ibid; 151

101 ibid; 152

iv. Other reasons of abrogation being confirmed in the contract[102]

v. Reorganisation of the enterprise because of a possible business failure, and respectively serious manufacturing or business difficulties that result in obvious streamlining procedures[103]

The amount of the subsistence payment is determined in Shanghai according to the period of employment in a certain company. For each year attended, the employee is entitled to get a single month salary[104]. The staff membership for a different firm is normally not important.

For a working duration of less than twelve month, half a month salary is payable. The maximum of subsequent payment is limited on twelve month salaries. In the cases (2) and (4) (v) the payment accounts for at least a month salary[105].

In the case (4) (v) there is not a maximum limit of twelve month salaries compulsory[106].

In case of a non-business related working incapability, the employee is designated to get medical cost support of around three to six months salaries[107].

3.4.9 Working time, recuperation days and vacation

Most of the Chinese work six days a week. In some sectors, especially in the building industry even seven days a week. In order to guarantee an improvement of this situation, the following regulations came into effect.

Working Time

Weekly working Time: According to the Labour Law, the maximum working time is set at 44 hours[108]. Already after five month of

[102] ibid; 152
[103] cp. Labour Law of the PRC; Art. 28
[104] cp. Das Recht der Investitionen in China; Andreas Diem; p. 152
[105] ibid; p. 152
[106] ibid; p. 152
[107] ibid; p. 152

having published the Law, the State Council released a regulation, whereby the average working time was limited on 40 hours[109].

Daily working Time: The daily working time should not exceed the limit of eight hours[110]. But it is allowed to surpass this limitation in a modest way. In that occasion the working staff and the Union have to be heard. However, an approval from these two parties is not needed. In emergency cases, it is even allowed to ignore and skip the hearing procedure[111].

Overtime work: Working hours that are fulfilled outside of the regular working time, are classified as overtime work. Overtime work can be cleared by additional leisure time[112], or have to paid off in a monetary way after a strict scale designed for extra working hours.

For the fulfilling of an extra working hour on a weekday, 150 % are retaliated. On a recuperation day, 200 % of the normal bases have to be retaliated. During the vacation time, 300 % are designated[113].

Recuperation and anniversary days

Recuperation days: Since the May 1, 1995 has the Chinese week only five working days. Two days serve as recuperation days[114]. Normally it is Saturday and Sunday. If a company cannot abide by this rule because of production schedules, it has the possibility to get an exception at the Labour administration concerning this regulation[115]. There are eight national holidays[116]. On the recuperation and anniversary days the loan or wages are paid[117].

---

108 cp. Labour Law of the PRC; Art. 36

109 cp. Das Recht der Investitionen in China; Andreas Diem; p. 153

110 cp. Labour Law of the PRC; Art. 36

111 ibid; Art. 41/42

112 ibid; Art. 44 para 2

113 ibid; Art. 44

114 ibid; Art. 38

115 ibid; Art. 39

116 ibid; Art. 40

117 ibid; Art. 51

Vacation

There are two different types of vacation: A recovering holiday, to which everybody is entitled, and a special leave day, that can be applied for under certain circumstances.

Recovering holiday

An employee, who has worked a year in a row, has a legitimate claim for a recovery holiday[118]. This claim has originally been regulated throughout national and local regulations. In many state owned enterprises, the core amount of the employees or workers do not get a single vacation day in the first five years of employment. The practical behaviour within foreign invested companies varies very strongly.

Allowance of special leave: A company, which benefits its employees with voluntarily paid recovering vacation, has the permission to reduce this vacation claim by the amount of legitimate anniversary days and the special leave.

Legitimate special leave

Marriage vacation: A male, who has not reached his 25th birthday, and a woman who has not reached her 23rd birthday and if both of them get married for the first time in their lives, they are entitled to get five days of paid vacation. If they marry later, the claim for additional paid vacation raises up to ten days[119].

Maternity leave: Maternity vacation has to be granted for at least 90 days[120]. The holiday starts 15 days prior to giving birth, and ends 75 days after[121]. In case of complications or multiple births, the vacation can be prolonged.

---

118 ibid; Art. 45 para 2

119 cp. Das Recht der Investitionen in China; Andreas Diem; p. 154

120 cp. Labour Law of the PRC; Art. 62

121 cp. Das Recht der Investitionen in China; Andreas Diem; p. 154

In Shanghai, there also exists a prolonged vacation period, if the mother has already had her 24th birthday. In that occasion, also the father is entitled to get three free days[122]. During the maternity leave, the complete wage is being paid.

Family vacations: A married employee, who lives divorced from his or her partner and an unmarried employee who lives separated from his or her parents, has claim for 20 - 30 days, including weekend and anniversary days, to get retaliated special leave. Married employees, who are living apart from their parents, are allowed to visit them every fourth year for twenty days. It is assumed, that a worker or employee is living separated form his parents, if he or she is not capable to reach them within one day by using the train.

Treatment vacation: A worker in Shanghai, who did not become ill because of job-related issues or has suffered an accident, has the right to get treatment vacation.

Others: Moreover, there is special leave days provided in the cases of death or for sterilisation[123].

3.4.10 Wages

Employees: The employer has the unrestricted freedom to determine the wage level[124]. This rule applies also for foreign invested enterprises. Whenever a foreign invested enterprise is founded, the wage structure is determined by the administration board, with the requirement, that the wage structure does not lie below the Chinese average of 100% native companies[125]. The mark-up of wages is enacted by the administration board or negotiated with the union or working staff[126]. The rule that foreign invested companies have to pay 20 % more than local Chinese companies of the same in the line business has been abolished.

---

[122] cp. Das Recht der Investitionen in China; Andreas Diem; p. 155
[123] cp. Labour Law of the PRC; Art. 51
[124] ibid; Art. 47
[125] cp. Das Recht der Investitionen in China; Andreas Diem; p. 155
[126] cp. Das Recht der Investitionen in China; Andreas Diem; p. 155

But since 1995 a minimum wage system exists[127]. The minimum level is determined by the administrations of the provinces, autonomous regions and municipalities. The monthly minimum wage lies in Shanghai at a level below 50 Euros.

Expatriates: There is the policy "same income for same work"128. This principle is not applicable on employees overseas. The expatriates have already had a much higher income at their affiliate in the source country. They usually expect a bonus payment in addition to that for their engagement in China. To justify this behaviour and apply to this principle by the same token, the Ministry of Labour has created the following solution.

If a joint-venture employs Chinese and overseas senior management personnel at the same time, and the wages are remunerated by the foreign firm, then the Chinese management is paid by a nominal-real wage system[129]. The nominal wage, which relates to an accordant foreign executive wage, is determined by the administration board of the foreign invested enterprise[130].

The actual earnings of the Chinese executive are determined by the Chinese joint-venture partner and the accordant technical authority. The wage level should be appropriate for local standards[131]. Only the actual wage is remunerated to the Chinese executive. The difference between nominal wage and actual earnings are channelled into additional social insurances and the companies' welfare and housing funds. The union supervises the capital[132]. The Chinese has to pay taxes only on his actual earnings[133].

Taking a wholly-foreign owned enterprise, a nominal-real wage system does not exist. The wholly-foreign owned enterprise has to pay categorically comparable wages to both, the Chinese and the overseas executive. But the expatriate can ask for additional payment covering moving, apartment, school fees and so forth. Moreover, he is entitled to get living abroad allowance. In real life,

---

127 cp. Labour Law of the PRC; Art. 48
128 cp. Das Recht der Investitionen in China; Andreas Diem; p. 156
129 ibid; p. 156
130 ibid; p. 156
131 cp. Das Recht der Investitionen in China; Andreas Diem; p. 156
132 ibid; p. 156
133 ibid; p. 156

there are a score of solutions. The infringement of the principle "same income for same work" is not punishable.

3.4.11 Illness and accident

Illness and accident not related to business activities

A worker or employee in Shanghai, who does not get ill because of a job-related activity or has suffered an accident, is entitled to get treatment vacation and continuation of payments.

Treatment vacation: During the legitimate treatment vacation the employer must not dismiss the employee. The dismissal is only allowed after the treatment vacation and the compliance with the 30 days notice period[134].

The maximum treatment period depends on employment time so far. The chart below displays the relation between fulfilled working time and the concerning treatment period that is compulsory for the employer to offer[135].

Figure 3: Relation between working time and treatment period

Completed duration treatment	**Period of**	**Period of**
of employment	**current employment**	**vacation**
Under 10 years	under 5 years	3 months
	under 10 years	6 months
10 to 20 years	under 5 years	6 months
	5 to 10 years	9 months
	10 to 15 years	12 months
	15 to 20 years	18 months
Over 20 years	under 5 years	12 months
	5 to 10 years	18 months
	10 to 15 years	24 months
determined	Over 15 years	not

Continuation of payment: During the first six months of the treatment vacation, the wage is remunerated in the subsequent levels:

---

134 ibid; p. 157
135 ibid; p. 157

Figure 4: Continuation of payment I

Completed duration of employment	Continuation of Payment by taking 70% of actual earnings as basis
Under 2 years	60 %
2 to 4 years	70 %
4 to 6 years	80 %
6 to 8 years	90 %
Over 8 years	100 %

After expiration of the first six months until the end of the legitimate treatment vacation, is the wage only paid in accordance to the following chart:

Figure 5: Continuation of payment II

Complete duration of employment	Continuation of Payment by taking 70% of the actual earnings as basis
Under 1 year	40 %
1 to 3 years	50 %
Over 3 years	60 %

Business-related illness and working accident

If a worker or employee gets ill because of job-related activities or suffers from a work accident and thus leads to a condition that enables that certain person to only achieve the goals to certain extend, then the employer is allowed to dismiss this employee[136]. A worker that is classified 1 to 4 on a scale from 1 to 10 "should" resign and hand in his termination note[137]. The first degree is the highest point of non-capability to exercise the duty, 10 is the lowest degree. The actual degree of working non-capability is determined by the local Labour Assessment Commission.

3.4.12 Non-competition clause

An employee who got into contact with business secrets or sensitive know-how can be exposed to a non-competition clause. This certain

[136] cp. Das Recht der Investitionen in China; Andreas Diem; p. 158
[137] ibid; p. 158

employee is accordingly not allowed to work for another company of the same in the line business for at least two years. The range of products and the function of his or her former job should not be related to the new working place. Further more, the employee has no permission to manufacture or distribute the products and commodities on his own he or she had contact with during the last occupation. The core objective is to impede the possibility of this former employee to get into direct competition with his former employer[138]. The non-competition clause must not exceed the period of three years. The former employer has to pay compensation. The amount of compensation is not determined.

3.4.13 Particular protection for female and minor employees

There are some employment prohibitions[139] and limitations for female workers, especially during pregnancy and lactation[140] as well as during the period of the mentioned 90 days of maternity leave[141]. Minor workers between 16 and 18 are not allowed to get assigned to certain employments[142]. The employment of employees under 16 is generally not permitted in the companies. Exceptions are possible for art, sports or activities that require special skills and knowledge[143].

3.5 Labour disputes

For the settlement of labour disputes a three-stage procedure is scheduled. The first step is the mediation in front of the settlement commission of the company[144]. The settlement commission consists of labour representatives, officials from the employer's site and the union. The union selects the head of commission[145].

If the whole procedure does not lead to an agreement, every party is allowed to request an arbitration procedure within 60 days in front

---

138 ibid; p. 159
139 cp. Labour Law of the PRC; Art. 59
140 ibid; Art. 60/61/63
141 ibid; Art. 62
142 ibid; Art. 64
143 cp. Labour Law of the PRC; Art. 15
144 ibid; Art. 79
145 ibid; Art. 80

of the Arbitration Commission for Labour Disputes[146]. In Shanghai it is the Shanghai Labour Administration Commission. The arbitration Commission implies representatives of the Labour administration, the local Union organisation and one employer. The head of commission is appointed by the labour administration[147].

If one of the parties does not accept the judgement, the complaining party has the possibility to file an action to an ordinary court[148], within 15 days[149] after receiving the written arbitration. The rules and regulations are basically applied to any disputes in connection with collectivistic contracts of employment[150].

3.6 Unions and collective agreement

In Germany, the unions form the backbone of the domestic workforce in terms of negotiation power towards the employers. The organizational character is outstanding and German unions are perceived among the most powerful worldwide. In the subsequent section this thesis will elaborate on the prevalent situation in China until today and reflects the main differences to the Union character in Western societies.

3.6.1 Trade Union Law from 1992

The Trade Union law was already forty years old when the Central Committee decided to implement a new labour code in regard to this issue[151]. The main points of the reformations appointed educational measures; entailing work discipline, work moral, retraining and the support of the ongoing economic growth of the PRC[152] (we will later on take a closer look on this point). In the following we will describe the main regulations of the Trade Union Law from 1992.

---

146 ibid; Art. 82
147 ibid; Art. 81
148 ibid; Art. 79
149 ibid; Art. 83
150 cp. Labour Law of the PRC; Art. 84
151 See Arbeit in China; Rolf Geffken; p. 64
152 See Arbeit in China; Rolf Geffken; p. 65

The Unions' task is to represent the employees and safeguard their rights and interests[153]. The term "Union" (Chinese: gong hui) is not comparable to the German sense of meaning. The Chinese Labour Law perceives any representative association founded by workers to be a union.

Unions can be launched by a single company, or get an interplanetary character by representing whole regions or industrial sectors[154]. A union is an entity or corporate body. The employees have the right to found a union, but not the duty to do so[155].

Rights: The union has the right, to participate at meetings of the board of administration without having any influence on the decision-making process. Issues concerning business plans as well as employee's punishment or rewards can be part of these meetings[156]. The union can clinch contracts in the name of the working staff concerning collective contracts of employment with the employer[157]. Owner ship rights are very limited in the Chinese Law.

The unions usually have the allowance only to get a hearing. The union is not capable to block decisions or even have the right to co-decide. Unions can advocate for objection, if they do not agree with a dismissal. But the objection does not have any legal consequences[158]. If a union perceives a dismissal to be unjustified, because of legal or regulatory reasons, then it can force the employer to deal with this certain incident again[159].

Support: The employer shall provide the union with facilities and office supplies[160]. Moreover, the employer has to pay in into the Union Fund[161]. The payments add up to 2 % of the complete wages being remunerated to the working staff within a foreign directed enterprise[162].

---

153 cp. Labour Law of the PRC; Art. 7
154 cp. Das Recht der Investitionen in China; Andreas Diem; p. 160
155 ibid; p. 160
156 ibid; p. 160
157 ibid; p. 161
158 ibid; p. 161
159 cp. Labour Law of the PRC; Art. 30
160 cp. Das Recht der Investitionen in China; Andreas Diem; p. 161
161 ibid; p.161
162 ibid; p.161

3.6.2 Collective contracts of employment

Companies and Unions have the fundamental right, but not the duty, to clinch collective contracts of employment[163]. A collective contract of employment - comparable to a company agreement - can entail regulations concerning remuneration, working time, recovering days, vacation, work safety and health care, social insurance and welfare[164]. This renumeration is not can be enlarged. Contract party on the worker's site is the union. The collective agreements have to be named at the Labour Administration. If the Labour Administration demurs, then collective contract of employment cannot be ratified. After becoming effective, individual contracts are not allowed to undermine the core benefits of the collective contract of employment[165].

3.6.3 The Union Law from 2001 and its practical experience

One of the improvements at that juncture was the regulation that nobody could be hindered to exert his union-related activities[166] and companies are not allowed to dismiss unions within their enterprises without having a good reason[167]. Moreover, each company with more than 25 employees is designated to found a workers' representation[168]. Further more, a company union congress is appointed to elect the members of the company union committee which directly deals with the worker's related issues[169].

Practical experience however shows that elections for the company union committee take seldom place. But the ACFTU is increasing its efforts to bring elections on its way. If elections take place, some members can possibly origin even from subordinate departments[170].

In the version of 2001 it is granted for the first time that full-time and part-time functionaries can be appointed. By the same token,

---

163 cp. Labour Law of the PRC; Art. 33
164 ibid; Art. 33
165 ibid; Art. 35
166 cp. Trade Union Law of the PRC (2001); Art. 3
167 ibid; Art. 12
168 ibid; Art. 10
169 http://www.woek-web.de/.../publikationen/heuer_2004_vr_china _das_novellierte_gewerkschaftsgesetz.pdf; cp. Arbeitsrecht26.pdf; p. 2/3
170 ibid; Cp. Arbeitsrecht26.pdf; p. 3

the period of contract of employment is extended to the full period as union representative[171]. This enables union functionaries to exert their task with a higher degree of efficiency. Part-time functionaries have the right to spent three days a month for union activities by continuation of payments[172]. The head of a company union can only be dismissed if more than 50% of all company union congress members agree[173].

Practical experience concerning this point still reflects that company union representatives, members of the corresponded human resource department and the local labour bureaus still have tight connections and a strong influence on the company union congresses. For instance, a company union congress still does not have the power to prevent the dismissal from union functionaries or hamper a displacement procedure[174].

The improvements form 2001 also allows unions initially to represent and safeguard the interest of the employees[175] and declares it as one of the basic duties of the unions[176]. It is also emphasized that anyone can become a member of a union[177]. Article four of the Trade Union Law of the PRC states however that trad unions have to act in accordance with economic growth and must not impede this development. Caroline Heuer, an expert on this field quotes that the union needs to be regarded as an instrument of economic development[178]. Unions are legitimized to take court action if their work is impeded[179].

Taking a closer look at the practical experience of this controversial issue, we have to point out that company unions still do not take actions to improve the workers' situations. The staffs often do not even now about the existence of a company union or the legitimate right to found such an organization. There is still the widespread

---

[171] cp. Trade Union Law of the PRC (2001); Art. 18

[172] ibid; Art. 40

[173] ibid; Art. 17

[174] http://www.woek-web.de/.../publikationen/heuer_2004_vr_china _das_novellierte_gewerkschaftsgesetz.pdf; See Arbeitsrecht26.pdf; p. 4

[175] cp. Trade Union Law of the PRC (2001); Art. 2

[176] ibid; Art. 6

[177] ibid; Art. 3

[178] http://www.woek-web.de/.../publikationen/heuer_2004_vr_china _das_novellierte_gewerkschaftsgesetz.pdf; See Arbeitsrecht26.pdf; p. 4/5

[179] cp. Trade Union Law of the PRC (2001); Art. 49

opinion that existing unions do often cooperate with the executives of the respective cooperation. In further chapters this thesis will elaborate on that point more precisely.

However, there has been no case reported in which a company union instituted legal proceedings[180].

Collective agreements which set the framework of rights to protect the work staff are still determined or signed only few and far between. Pursuant to Article 20 of the Trade Union Law, the Union is allowed to call a court in case of violation of the collective agreement. However, this right is very seldom applied[181] .

There have been actions undertaken to improve the negotiation position of the unions. Since 2001, unions can participate at negotiation rounds including the company executives and the local labour office[182].

Practical experience differed also in this occasion heavily from the theoretical possibilities of the union activists. There is a clear hierarchical structure. Company decisions are made by the enterprises management. Outside the enterprise, labour office decisions are valid[183].

The Union Law gives Chinese workers to co-determinate regulations, guidelines and statutes concerning the work environment. They are also designated to co-determine the work schedule[184]. The Law body from 2001 alters the role of the union in a remarkable sense. The union is not anymore responsible to the company's management, but for the company's success. In addition to that, the company union is allowed to access the firms' supervisory board[185]. Pursuant to Article 23 of the Trade Union Law, company executives should seriously consider the unions' proposals and more than that. Article 25 of the Trade Union Law appoints the union to investigate worker's rights violations by getting all the

---

180 http://www.woek-web.de/.../publikationen/heuer_2004_vr_china _das_novellierte_gewerkschaftsgesetz.pdf; See Arbeitsrecht26.pdf; p. 5

181 http://www.woekweb.de/.../publikationen/heuer_2004_vr_china _das_novellierte_gewerkschaftsgesetz.pdf; See Arbeitsrecht26.pdf; p. 6

182 cp. Trade Union Law of the PRC (2001); Art. 34

183 http://www.woek-web.de/.../publikationen/heuer_2004_vr_china_ das_novellierte_gewerkschaftsgesetz.pdf; See Arbeitsrecht26.pdf; p. 6

184 cp. Trade Union Law of the PRC (2001); Art. 33/34

185 ibid; Art. 39

support and assistance required. In case of strike, the position of the union has markedly been altered to the version of 1992. Before 2001 the union was expected to settle the dispute together with head of the company. Starting 2001, the union is clearly positioned on the employee's end[186].

Experiences so far showed that union representatives are not usually accepted that well. They are often not perceived to be on the same negotiation level as the cooperation executives[187].

The Trade Union Law from 2001 gives company unions an important role during the process of settlement of labour disputes. There are three different steps designated. The first level of labour dispute resolution demands for the creation of an arbitration panel within the company. The 2nd level expects an arbitration panel consisting of the union representatives, company executives and members of the labour office to search for a solution. If this is not the case, the union has the right to appear before court[188].

Practical experience displays however a pretty clear situation that speaks in favour of the employers. Agreements are normally realized by the company executives or the local labour office. In case of a trial, the decision is normally dictated by the central governments[189].

The type of business ownership determines on an official level the activities and duties of a union. However, practical experience has displaying a growing identical character of the company's unions. There are still significant differences in the organizational structure of the unions. State-owned enterprises have very well-organized unions, private owned enterprises still reflect a remarkable lack of organization. The organizational efficiency of unions in joint-ventures depends on the origin of the joint-venture partner. The ACFTU monitors especially Asian-originated ventures, because minimum standards are mostly violated by them[190].

---

186 ibid; Art. 27

187 http://www.woek-web.de/.../publikationen/heuer_2004_vr_china_das_novellierte_gewerkschaftsgesetz.pdf; See Arbeitsrecht26.pdf; p. 9

188 cp. Trade Union Law of the PRC (2001); Art. 28

189 http://www.woek-web.de/.../publikationen/heuer_2004_vr_china_das_novellierte_gewerkschaftsgesetz.pdf; See Arbeitsrecht26.pdf; p. 9

190 ibid; See Arbeitsrecht26.pdf; p. 11

Union contribution payments can be sued by the union[191]. In fact, companies do only transmit very seldom union contributions to the unions. Only in regions in which the density of joint-ventures is high, union are financially supported on a regular basis[192].

3.6.4 Conclusion

There is no doubt that unions play an important role in a country's political landscape. Caroline Scheuer has stated unions in China find themselves in a difficult situation; they are part of the official union (ACFTU) and union structure[193]. The party is careful to ensure that the trade union comes under tighter surveillance than other bureaucracies[194]. This leads to an inherent lack of effective results. The reasons go hand in hand with little or not specified definitions of rights. She clearly names the election process of official union members which has to be more specified in terms of eligibility and electivity. She adds that the number of committee members has to be determined and the right for strikes needs to get more detailed as well. The mentioned controversial issues clearly reflect that unions in China will have difficulties to gain a noticeable position in labour relations[195]. In chapter seven, this thesis will elaborate on the latest improvements of the Trade Union Law in China.

3.7 The Local implementation of the Employment Contract System

This section will deal with the actual practice of the reforms. We will highlight which difficulties emerged and had to be faced by the labour administration and industrial enterprises in implementing policies imposed by the central government. From actual practice, one may abstract a paradigm of administrative rule-making and rule application in China[196].

---

191 cp. Trade Union Law of the PRC (2001); Art. 43

192 http://www.woek-web.de/.../publikationen/heuer_2004_vr_china _das_novellierte_gewerkschaftsgesetz.pdf; See Arbeitsrecht26.pdf; p. 11

193 http://www.chinapolitik.de/studien/china_analysis/no_45.pdf; See Arbeitsrecht09.pdf; p. 24

194 Cp. Der chinesische Arbeitsmarkt; Anita Chan; p. 253

195 http://www.chinapolitik.de/studien/china_analysis/no_45.pdf; See Arbeitsrecht09.pdf; p. 25

196 cp. Labour Law in China; Hillary K. Josephs; p. 48

3.7.1 National objectives vs. priorities of local governments

The Implementation of the Contract Employment System has followed the "top down" approach, a pattern typically used for policy initiatives. The top level of the central government unseals an initiative without necessarily having checked all the possible repercussions of the initiative. The central government usually expects the local government to find solutions for the specific issues that need to be solved[197].

Many sectors of the Chinese economy have been traditionally directed by the central government, but the allocation of manpower has developed primarily as operative area or responsibility area for local government officials. Labour bureaus were always responsible for the detailed allocation procedures. The Contract Employment system was introduced only very slowly and it was already clear at the beginning that in the long run only implementation could be successful[198].

One of the paramount factors behind the slow implementation of the Contract Employment System is the instrumental approach with bureaucrats adopt toward policy initiatives. Local bureaucrats show real aversion to implementation procedure if they go hand in hand with costs that are not compensated by the central government. The less beneficial the whole implementation is expected to be the less is the effort undertaken by local officials to establish the new system.

By introducing the Contract Employment System to its full extent the local bureaucrats expect the following downsides[199]:

(1) Higher levels of unemployment → rising costs

(2) Dismissals might provoke greater number of labour disputes, thus leads to a higher degree of social unrest and rising costs

(3) Local managers lose face by dismissing obsolete employees → leads to social tensions, including possible riots and turmoils

---

197 cp. Labour Law in China; Hillary K. Josephs; p. 49

198 See Der chinesische Arbeitsmarkt; Jutta Hebel Jude Howell; p. 139

199 cp. Labour Law in China; Hillary K. Josephs; p. 50/51

Due to these aspects, the implementation came only very slowly into effect. In addition, the central government showed reluctance to use pressure in order to force cooperation from their subordinates (concept of losing face)[200].

The government is aware of the fact that it only has limited influence concerning job allocation matters. However, there is not another project that is promulgated with such purposefulness. Main points of interest are the abolishment of permanent employment and the custom of state enterprise workers to get replaced by their own children[201].

The central government often quoted Article 100 of the Constitution, which implies that local governments may enact laws only to the extent that they do not conflict with national laws and regulations.[202] Until today, local governments did never challenge national directives[203]. Nonetheless, local agencies have expressed their opposition to the contract employment system from time to time either by issuing contrary regulations or by exploiting loopholes or ambiguities in the national regulations. Eventually, such local resistance was successful and national law was amended to accommodate local concerns[204].

3.7.3 The Contract Employment System and its local implementation

This section will deal with cities or municipalities of Beijing, Shenzhen and Shanghai, which were the first areas to introduce the Contract Employment System and its experiences. These metro poles were chosen due to their low level of unemployment and relative prosperity resilience. Initiatives were already launched in the early 1980s

---

200 http://resources.alibaba.com/article/2492/Concepts_in_Chinese_culture.htm; See Arbeitsrecht11.pdf; p. 1

201 cp. Labour Law in China; Hillary K. Josephs; p. 52

202 http://english.people.com.cn/constitution/constitution.html; See Arbeitsrecht12.pdf; p. 16

203 cp. Labour Law in China; Hillary K. Josephs; p. 53

204 ibid; p. 54

Implementation in the capital of China: Beijing

Beijing reflects an excellent illustration of the ability of powerful local government to string the central government policy along while meeting the expectations of local interest groups at the same time. This situation is the reason why the implementation was not effectively applied from 1982 – 1988.

The full implementation took so long, because the Beijing Labour Bureau shrank away from intensified hiring difficulties. Also the enterprises themselves were reluctant to hire people under the contract employment system and still preferred to replace their workers by their children. At that juncture the most obvious problem to be dealt with was to find job alternatives of redundant permanent workers[205].

Further more, the contract employment was likely to promote labour mobility among skilled and technical workers; the group enterprises would have the most difficulty replacing them. The Beijing labour authorities had already tried to accommodate enterprises in this regard, by authorizing both long-term contracts (five to ten years) and contracts of unlimited duration. Additionally, skilled workers who wanted to leave their working place before expiration of the contract of employment had to pay a so-called "training fee" to their former employer in order to remunerate his efforts to train the worker. Although Beijing has a vibrant, viable and diversified economy and is considered one of the most desirable places in China to live, individual firms hoard skilled manpower and receive the support of the local labour authorities in doing so[206].

Implementation in Shanghai

Shanghai has long been China's most important industrial city, in terms of output, exports, and revenues paid to the central government. After a slow start, economic reform picked up remarkable velocity. By the end of the 1990s, Shanghai had attracted substantial foreign investment and thus Shanghai currently accounts for eight per cent of total FDI in China (2007: 52.4 billion

[205] cp. Labour Law in China; Hillary K. Josephs; p. 55/56
[206] ibid; p. 57

Euros) and 25 % of all exports go through Shanghai harbour[207]. Shanghai capitalized on the growth of the adjacent provinces of Jiangsu and Zhejiang. State enterprises in Shanghai entered into profitable subcontracting arrangements with these newly established businesses in the interior, which enjoyed lower costs of production. Secretary Jiang Zemin and Vice Premier Zhu Rongji, originally coming form Shanghai, used their political influence to promote the city's prosperity.

Restructuring the labour bureau policies in Shanghai was less problematic than in Beijing. The industrial power of the city made it possible to implement the Contract Employment System far easier than in the capital. However, there were also regulations that discouraged local employees to change their working places. For instance: a worker in Shanghai enjoyed usually paid sick leave. But the period of payment was closely tied to the duration of work with a single employer. The longer an employee had worked for an employer the longer he was designated to receive paid sick leave[208]. This means that the loyalty to a single employer went hand in hand with the amount of beneficial payments.

Implementation in Shenzhen

Shenzhen is a very young city in terms of intense urbanization. Located along the border to Hong Kong, it was elevated from a rural county to a municipality under the Guangdong provincial government in 1979. In the same year, a substantial portion of the city was designated a Special Economic Zone ("SEZ"). This gave the impetus to Hong Kong firms to shift their manufacturing activities to Shenzhen and other SEZs of the Guangdong province to benefit from lower labour and land costs, while concentrating locally on high-end production activities and services. The city developed also very quickly in terms of population and economic power. From formerly 30.000 citizens to officially 1.5 million today and was capable to multiply its GDP by 1800 times to 42.2 million Euros[209].

---

207 http://www.export.gov/china/shanghaicontacts.asp; SeeArbeits-recht13.pdf; p. 1

208 cp. Labour Law in China; Hillary K. Josephs; p. 59

209 http://www.newsgd.com/news/guangdong1/200608310078.htm; See Arbeitsrecht15.pdf

From the beginning, the Chinese government treated Shenzhen as a model of rapid economic development and a greenfield to demonstrate Chinese enterprises, the superiority of the Contract Employment System to the permanent employment system[210].

However, in the realm of employment relations, Shenzhen has not been a "laboratory for change" which could be – or should be- copied elsewhere in China. Although some of the systems implemented, were pretty influential for the rest of the country. The wage system of the early 1980s for instance, was often used as a role model for further wage systems [211] However, the predominant management style in Shenzhen is abusive and exploitative, a regression to the kind of factory operations which inspired Marxism in the first place[212]. Labour dispute cases have skyrocketed from 56 reported cases in 1986, to 13.280 in 1999[213] for instance.

In the early 1980s, ordinary workers were commonly recruited through arrangements between Shenzhen government labour service company and labour bureaus in areas of Guangdong province where a labour surplus existed. Local labour bureaus and enterprise employees who were in charge to hire new workers went to Guangdong province to recruit or hire employees. Commonly, the local labour bureau got paid a "service fee" for their efforts.

Skilled and specialized workers were hired differently, normally throughout newspaper advertisements and temporary transfer from other work units.

Thus, with the maturation of the local economy, the Shenzhen government has adopted the same attitude of local protectionism as Beijing and Shanghai. It imposes controls on the size of the permanent resident population, maintaining a society strictly bifurcated between locals and outsiders. Recent regulations set minimum quotas for local hires and prohibit lay-offs of local resident. Companies which do not meet their quotas or which lay off residents are subject to fines. As a result, those with temporary residence status, even if they have several years of meritorious service with the firm, are subject to retrenchment[214].

---

210 cp. Labour Law in China; Hillary K. Josephs; p. 61

211 See Der chinesiche Arbeitsmarkt; Jutta Hebel Jude Howell; page 140

212 cp. Labour Law in China; Hillary K. Josephs; p. 62

213 See Against the Law; Ching Kwan Lee; p. 7

214 cp. Labour Law in China; Hillary K. Josephs; p. 64/65

3.7.4 Conclusion and current situation

To the extent that policies such as contract employment were intended to work an incremental but fundamental transformation in the system of employment, the new regulations have not achieved the main objectives. The legal situation, governing employment has not radically changed since the late 1970s[215].

Labour practices in large-scale, capital-intensive foreign invested enterprises (FIEs) tend to duplicate those in state enterprises. In general, the Chinese government prefers that FIEs take on as many social welfare obligations as possible, including unemployment insurance, health care and other social welfare benefits in a manner similar to state-owned enterprises[216].

The elimination of job assignments, the growth of the non-state sector, and the development of alternative employment opportunities produced positive effects for the individual and the state. However, the contract employment system has not completely arrived at the state enterprises: Compensation based on seniority and a paternalistic management style is still predominant[217]. This aspect is interesting for FIEs that are looking for a joint-venture partner in China. Cases report that the Western or overseas joint-venture partner had to employ the pre-existing workforce of the Chinese company. Even the farmers that lived on the area of the factory had to be recruited[218].

A definite downside is that the emergence of labour markets has given rise to forms of worker exploitation and discrimination which were suppressed under a system of job assignment. Unskilled workers are mainly target of these exploitation activities[219]. Further more, the process of conversion did not take place overnight. By the end of 1997, only about half of a state enterprise workforce was under contract[220]. It surpassed the 75% mark in 1999 compared to 23

---

[215] ibid; p. 65

[216] ibid; p. 66

[217] See On the Use of Incentive Pay in Chinese State-owned Enterprises: The Role of Hierarchy; Frank Bodmer; p. 26

[218] See Der Chinesiche Arbeitsmarkt; Jude Howell; p. 139

[219] See Against the Law; Ching Kwan Lee; p. 43

[220] cp. Labour Law in China; Hillary K. Josephs; p. 67

% in non-state sectors[221]. State enterprises are not allowed to lay off employees in the western sense. They are expected to redeploy surplus workers internally through "reemployment service centres"[222].

But the globalization trend also urges state enterprise managers to improve productivity. FDI enterprises have picked up and are more efficient than state owned enterprises. The industrial output of state enterprises has plummeted from 75% to 26% in 1997[223]. The mere presence of greater number of temporary workers, even if they are relegated to menial and unskilled tasks, creates apprehension in the permanent workforce. Wages have gone up since the early 1980s; inflation erodes the value of wage and pensions increases[224].

In fact, at this juncture the Ministry of Labour and Social Security (successor organisation of the Ministry of Labour since 1998[225]) and the Ministry of Personnel do not assign people to specific jobs. However, they monitor the employment relationship very closely. Wages and fringe benefits of state enterprise employees and civil servants are still set by administrative regulation. Like other ministries in China, the Ministry of Labour and Social Security seizes every new opportunity to expand its regulatory reach. It has done recently, for example, with respect to the use of the Internet as a recruitment device. The Ministry of Labour and Social Security and local labour bureaus have discovered that it is not necessary to exercise micromanagement in every respect in order to maintain the degree of control which they deem minimally necessary at a given stage of economic development[226]. From this perspective, the local implementation has still a long way to go and will probably never be amended to its full extension. Regional governments, autonomous regions and municipalities will always try to realize their personal local interests.

---

221 See Against the Law; Ching Kwan Lee; p. 239

222 cp. Labour Law in China; Hillary K. Josephs; p. 67

223 cp. Against the Law; Ching Kwan Lee; p. 39

224 cp. Labour Law in China; Hillary K. Josephs; p. 68

225 http://www.gov.cn/english/2005-10/02/content_74185.htm; See Arbeitsrecht17.pdf

226 cp. Labour Law in China; Hillary K. Josephs; p. 69

4. Cases

This section will discuss the situation in Chinese foreign invested companies and law violations that took place in those companies. This chapter will name the core violations amended by the employers and show, that the Chinese Labour Law has specific regulations that should encounter these grievances.

4.1 Shanghai Otis Elevator Company Ltd.

Liu Jianfa v. Shanghai Otis Elevator Company – Unfair Dismissal

Plaintiff: Liu Jianfa, male, 39 years old

Defendant: Shanghai Otis Elevator Company Ltd.

Plaintiff Liu Jianfa was originally employed by the Shanghai Branch of China Tianjin Otis Elevator Company. He signed an employment contract of unlimited duration with Tianjin Otis on October 21, 1989. On March 26, 1993 Tianjin Otis, Shanghai International Trust & Investment Company, and the Far East Group of Otis Company (U.S.A) signed a joint venture agreement, to establish Shanghai Otis Elevator Company. On June 1, Shanghai Otis was incorporated. On August 28, Shanghai Otis conducted its first board of directors meeting, resolved that the Shanghai branch of Tianjin Otis would cease operations, and announced its decision at the formal opening ceremony. Thereupon the workforce of the Shanghai branch, including Plaintiff, was absorbed into the workforce of Shanghai Otis, but Shanghai Otis neither terminated their existing employment contracts nor did it sign new employment contracts with them.

On November 16, Liu Jianfa was appointed manager of the installation department. On February 15, 1994, the management committee of Shanghai Otis removed Liu Jianfa from his position, alleging problems with quality control and engineering management. In the letter informing him of this decision, he was given two options:

(1) Submit a letter of resignation within four days, in which case he would receive four months salary and assistance in finding a new job

(2) In case of non-acceptance of point one, immediate dismissal

Liu did not submit a letter of resignation and was terminated; His reaction was to file a complaint with the Shanghai Labour Dispute Arbitration Committee. On January 26, 1994 Liu filed an appeal with the Huangpu District Court on February 9, 1995. In his appeal, Liu Jianfa argued that he had only served as manager of the installation department for three months and could not be blamed for several years of ongoing difficulties with quality control. Further more, the company had terminated him without consulting with the labour union, a violation of the procedural requirements of the labour law. He requested that his employment relationship with the company had to be restored.

In response, Shanghai Otis argued that it was not bound by the contract which Liu had signed with Tianjin Otis. It had not signed an employment contract with Liu and thus, according to local regulations, he was employed on a month-to-month basis. In lieu of one month's notice of termination, the company was willing to pay him one month's salary as severance. During his tenure, there had been many problems with quality control and the installation department was in sate of chaos. The image of the company had suffered accordingly. It was unaware of the existence of a labour union. Because of workplace rule violations and for other reasons, the company opposed reinstatement,

The Huangpu District Court found that the Shanghai Foreign Invested Enterprise Trade Union Federation had approved a change of name for the company union on June 26, 1993. The company had not consulted with union before terminating Liu. After he was terminated, the union had submitted written objection, but the company refused to accept it.

The court determined that all foreign invested enterprises are required to implement the Contract Employment System. Upon its establishment, Shanghai Otis had accepted all of the employees of the branch company. Even though it had not expressly terminated Liu's previous employment contract or signed a new contract with him. In practice the parties carried out their obligations under the original employment contact. Defendant's denial of an ongoing employment relationship does not comport with reality, in not consulting with union prior to terminating Liu, Shanghai Otis had acted contrary to fact and law. For these reasons, Liu's request for reinstatement should be granted. On June 19, 1995, pursuant to art. 10 (1) and art. 16 (1)(2) of the Shanghai Municipal Regulations on Labour Management in Sino-Foreign Joint Ventures, the court ordered that Liu be reinstated and that Shanghai Otis sign an employment contract with him

Shanghai Otis appealed the district court decision to the Second Intermediate Court. Shanghai Otis argued that it had not signed an employment contract with Liu and was not bound by the terms of his original contract with Tianjin Otis. When it discovered his dereliction of duty, it had the right to terminate the employment relationship. Further more, at that time, it was unaware of the existence of a trade union. The company's decision to terminate Liu should be sustained.

Liu argued that the parties had a de facto employment relationship which was an extension of the original contract, that he had not committed any dereliction of duty, and that Shanghai Otis had not sought approval for termination from the company union. The decision of the court of first instance should be affirmed.

Pursuant to art. 153 (1), first clause, of the Civil Procedure Law, the intermediate court decided that the district court was correct in its findings of fact. For the reasons stated in he proceedings below, it upheld the district court's decision and dismissed the appeal on September 27, 1995.

Commentary

The threshold issue in this case is whether plaintiff and defendant actually had an employment relationship, i.e., whether plaintiff was employed by defendant. Defendant argued in the first instance and on appeal that it had not signed a contract with plaintiff and that it was not bound by the contract between the now defunct branch company and plaintiff. In denying that an employment relationship existed, defendant's assertions were plainly in conflict with reality. Pursuant to art. 2 of the Labour Management Regulations for Chinese-Foreign Joint Ventures and art. 5 of the Implementing

Measures, joint ventures must practice the contract employment system. The parties must sign an employment contract and thereby establish an employment relationship.

The objective reality in this case is that the defendant failed to observe the necessary formalities. However, it is also true that if the defendant was established, it absorbed the workforce of the prior entity but it did not sign new employment contracts with them. The employer changed but the employees did not. Thus the original employment contracts continued in full force and effect. According to civil law theory, though one party to a contract may undergo a change of corporate form in accordance with law, the rights and obligations of the original contact pass to the successor entity. Therefore, the court of first instance and the appellate court were correct in rejecting defendant's argument.

The next point is that the lawful rights and interest of Chinese-foreign joint ventures operating within the territory of the PRC are protected under art. 2 of the Joint Venture Regulations, but by the same token a joint venture must comply in every respect with relevant laws. This requirement applies likewise to labour management. In its investigation of a case involving termination of an employee, the court must first look into the matter of procedural regularity. In other words, no matter what the employer's mandated procedures. The employer bears the burden of proving that in making and carrying out its decision it was acting in accordance with its management rights, In this case, the employer did not comply with mandated procedure in two respects.

First by removing, the employee from his position, the employer attempted to coerce him into resigning against his will. Such intimidations are contrary to the concept of voluntary resignation. Secondly, the employer did not give one month's advance notice of termination to the employee and the union. When the union did object, the employer flatly refused to consider its views. The trade union is a mass organization charged with protecting workers' lawful rights and interests. According to the trade Union Law, it is specially charged with particular responsibilities, including matters involving termination and discipline. When the employer dismisses or disciplines a worker without giving necessary notice to the union, the decision has no legal validity.

The employer's argument that it was "unaware" of the existence of a union at the time it dismissed the employee is absurd. The company union was in existence and officially recognized from the very month that the company was incorporated. To argue otherwise is pure sophistry. Since a finding of procedural regularity is a necessary predicate to an examination of the substantive legality of the employer's decision, the court can void the decision on procedural grounds alone and order the employee be reinstated. Therefore, the decision on first and second instance was correct.

4.2 Li Kai Di Chang shoe manufacturer

Plaintiff: work staff / china labour watch

Defendant: Li Kai Di Chang shoe manufacturer[227]

This case deals with a major shoe manufacturer in the south east of China, in the city of Hongyuan. Around 4000 workers are working in this typical Chinese factory. The employees suffered from different kinds of exploitation for a long time. This included not only the aggressive and irresponsible behaviour of the supervisory board. The major grievances in the Li Kai Factory Number 5, which produces for New Balance (the 3rd largest athletic and leisure shoe producer in the U.S., most of its operations were off shored to China) were the following:

- Low wages, below subsistence level 24 RMB / day → 2, 40 Euro / day. The average income in this factory is representative for the majority of manufacturing sites in the whole of China. It has not improved over the last decade
- A worker protection committee with members appointed by the executives of the factory thus led to a decision-making process in favour of the enterprise policies. The established union is never independent and does not go along due to its legal definition
- Talking back to a supervisor will result in the loss of three days' wages

[227] http//.www.chinalaborwatch.com; See Arbeitsrecht08.pdf

- Everyone must do "their duty to keep the place clean and that every day the room is swept and mopped three times, also during the working shift"
- Worker's wishing to leave the gated factory compound has to pass the security guards when they return. The guards have the clear order to go through their belongings without taking the employees' privacy and dignity into account
- A score of female employees are under aged and therefore not allowed to work
- The regular working time of eight hours a day is regularly exceeded and not rewarded
- Gender, age, height, and province of origin discrimination
- Lack of maintenance and food quality supply
- Non-remuneration of pensions and other benefit rights

This listing encounters markedly the New Balance companies' slogan "In respect to the way we treat our workers, our motto is this: Open, Fair and Just"

According to the Chinese Labour Law Code from 1995, under aged people (aged below 16) are not allowed to exert a working position[228]. Discriminatory behaviour during employing procedures is strictly governed by the Chinese Labour Law Code. The referred article underpins that the conclusion and modification of a labour contract shall follow the principle of equality[229]. Concerning the low wage issue, we have to consider a few more aspects. The workers in the Li Kai Factory earn around 55 Euro a month, but only get their full wage paid in case they achieve their production goal. Further more, the employees have to pay for their accommodation within the factory compound, a monthly rent of around 120 RMB (twelve Euros). The earned wage diminishes even more, because the working staffs have to remunerate its own food supply. Taking all these costs into account, the common worker at this firm has to cope with around 400 RMB a month (40 Euro). According to Chinese Law, the level of wages shall be gradually raised on the basis of

[228] cp. Labour Law of the PRC (NPC 05.07.1994); Art. 15
[229] cp. Labour Law of the PRC (NPC 05.07.1994); Art. 17

economic development. Moreover, the state or local labour bureaus shall monitor over the total payroll[230].

Further more, the wage level should be characterised or determined by its production, business, and economic results[231]. Especially this point should be taken into account, as already mentioned, New Balance is one of the paramount players in the shoe manufacturing business. The Labour Law also states that the government should implement in cooperation with the regional governments and municipalities a minimum wage[232], an income that safeguards the subsistence level of living of the population[233].

Taking a closer look at the working hours, this case displays a remarkable violation of the Labour Law articles governing this issue. According to Law, a Chinese worker is not allowed to work more than eight hours a day and 44 hours a week[234].

In addition to that, if a worker is willing to do some over time work, then the employing unit should limit this extension of working time to no more than 36 hours per month[235] and supplementary remunerate the extra hours in an appropriate way[236].

Also the right of paid holidays and marriage is regularly denied and disregarded by the factory leadership. A Chinese native worker has the clear right to get remuneration during his vacancies[237], particularly during periods concerning funerals and marriage have to be respected and disbursed[238].

According to the case, the company does also infringe basic rights concerning retirement fees and further fringe benefits, including child-bearing. Employees of this enterprise do usually not get any retirement payments, monetary support in case of illness or injury and the like[239].

---

[230] ibid; Art. 46
[231] ibid; Art. 47
[232] ibid; Art. 48
[233] ibid; Art. 49 para .1
[234] ibid; Art. 36
[235] ibid; Art. 41
[236] ibid; Art. 44
[237] ibid; Art 45
[238] ibid; Art. 51
[239] cp. Labour Law of the PRC (NPC 05.07.1994); Art. 73

The most controversial point is the presence of the company's union. The so-called "worker protection committee" is imposed by the management of Li Kai factory and favours constantly the position of the executive board. The core duty to serve the employees and represent their position in case of emerging disputes is permanently violated by the enterprise. The main objective of the union should be safeguarding the legitimate rights, within the scope of their respective duties and responsibilities, supervise the introduction of laws and regulations on labour[240].

4.3 Beijing Olympics

In the following section we will deal with the upcoming event in 2008, the Beijing Olympics. It is estimated that the profit of the Olympics games will profoundly exceed any expectations. But also in this situation, the core amount of benefits will not reach the employees of the companies mainly capitalizing on this event. It is not only the monetary benefits that will not benefit the working staffs, in addition to that, many labour rights are being violated by the participating enterprises at this major sports event[241].

Plaintiff: Working Staff / International Trade Union Confederation / Play Fair

Defendant: Chosen Beijing Olympics Supplier Enterprises

Lekit Sationery Co., Ltd.

Yue Wing Cheong Light Products Co., Ltd.

Eagle Leather Products Company Ltd.

Mainland Headwear Holdings Limited

The named companies are situated or conduct business in the sportswear, toy, and electronic appliance sector. These enterprises are representative for business manners among Chinese companies all across the nation. This section will deal with law violations employees of the listed companies suffer from.

The figures found during the investigations in the year 2007 reflect that a vast majority of companies in the manufacturing sector

---

240 ibid; Art. 88

241 http//.www.playfair2008.org/docs/playfair_2008-report.pdf; See Arbeitsrecht10.pdf

employ or hire a multitude of under aged workers in order to save costs. This behaviour contravenes with the article 15 of the Labour Law[242]. Many of the children being employed are aged between 12 and 15 and are often acquired to fulfil the same tasks as their adult colleagues.

A further issue that was regularly violated by these companies was the fact that the allowed working time period was not respected, and usually outstripped. The workers at the assembling line usually have a twelve hour working day instead of the regulated eight hours provided by law[243].

Talking about over time work, the employees have to go to production facilities also during their weekends, including Sundays. Requested days off are regularly declined. The following chart displays a common working day schedule[244]:

Figure 6: Working day schedule

Time	Daily Schedule
6.45 am	Wake Up
7.00 – 715 am	Breakfast
7:15 – 7:30 am	Punch timecard
7:30 – 8:00 am	Morning assembly
8:00 – 12:00	Morning work session
12:00 – 1:15 pm	Lunch and rest break
1:15 – 1:30 pm	Punch timecard
1:30 – 5:30 pm	Afternoon work session
5:30 – 6:15 pm	Dinner
6:15 – 6:30 pm	Punch timecard
6:30 – 10:30 pm or 2 am	Overtime Session

Considering this schedule, we have to point out that it deeply exceeds the legal working time period. Further more, the extra working hours are not voluntarily, but binding and already fixed in the daily working schedule. According to Chinese Law, a worker has the right to determine by his own will when he or she wants to exert overtime work[245]. Some eighty hours of monthly work are possible. The working time periods even increase the closer the

242 cp. Labour Law of the PRC (NPC 05.07.1994); Art.15

243 ibid; Art 36

244 See Playfair.pdf

245 cp. Labour Law of the PRC (NPC 05.07.1994); Art 41

Beijing Olympics get. Although China has numerous laws and regulations protecting the workers' constitution and guard against excessive overtime, the rights are weakly enforced.

In addition to working very long hours, the local minimum wages are permanently disregarded and not remunerated to the work staffs. Concerning this matter, these companies do not pay the minimum wage to their employees, but a wage that extremely undermines the subsistence level. Also the compulsory over time working hours are not rewarded at all. Particular in the case of extra hours, the Chinese law clearly has set standards for compensation[246].

A further controversial point is the imposing of unreasonable fines and deductions from wages. Wages are deducted in case of arriving too late to work, or being absent during the working shift for longer than a little time period. There exists also disciplinary system of fines within these enterprises. It ranges form 20 RMB (Two Euros) for "minor" mistakes, including not cleaning the dormitory and the like, up to 50 RMB for "major" mistakes and 80 RMB for "unforgivable" mistakes. Sources claim, that even a small fraction of the factory rules result in severe punishments and fines. The employer has the right to scale back the remuneration of his employees, if the employing unit has a reason to undertake this kind of action[247]. But the major amount of the named reasons can be questioned and is often immoderate for Western standards.

Another violation of law that constantly appears is the fact that workers do not get any payments for social security issues and other legal employment benefits. Average workers with no special knowledge and skills do not get this kind of benefits, although the Chinese Labour Law clearly states[248] that any worker shall enjoy social security and insurance benefits at retirement. The Law clearly arbitrates illness or injury, disability due to work-related injury or occupational illness, unemployment and childbirth.

According to many workers the working conditions can often be described as hazardous and unacceptable. Many of the production facilities of these companies face a lack of safety protection installations. The Chinese Labour Law also regulates this issue

---

246 ibid; Art 44

247 ibid; Art. 91 Nr. 1

248 cp. Labour Law of the PRC (NPC 05.07.1994); Art. 73

pretty clearly; the employment units have to undertake appropriate measures to guarantee the safety of their workers, including protective closing or gear for the prevention of occupational illness[249].

A further point to discuss is the maternity leave assured by law. Pregnant workers are entitled for paid maternity leave. The period is limited to 90 days[250]. This point should be heavily considered, because the main amounts of workers operating at the assembly lines are females. This article places high value on the safety of the health of both, mother and child.

4.4 Commentary

Taking a closer look at these cases, the most characteristic point that is constantly violated is the non-availability of a powerful and influential workers' representation. Either they do not exist or are simply established and represented by executive-friendly functionaries. The clear task or duty of the union, to represent the workers, and undertake actions to improve the situation of the work staffs cannot be realized under these circumstances. The Chinese Law precisely postulates that a Chinese enterprise has the duty to set up a union that safeguards the legitimate rights and interest of labourers, and enable them to conduct independently their activities in accordance with the law[251].

The Chinese Labour Law Code from 1995 is very comprehensive and goes hand in hand with the major goals postulated by Western societies. However, we have to distinguish between foreign invested companies and completely domestic enterprises. Foreign firms have to abide by the regulations in order to conduct business successfully in China. The Central government monitors foreign entities more strictly and enforces more frequently legitimate rights of the employees[252]. This does not mean that Asian investors are the only violators of the Labour Law regulations. In the recent past, cases have been reported in which Western enterprises generated profits

---

249 ibid; Art. 30

250 ibid; Art. 62

251 ibid; Art. 7

252 See Investment in China: A Question and Answer Guide on How to Do Business; Wang Yongjun; p. 143

by taking advantage of their Chinese employees. One of the most famous enterprises that are currently facing harsh criticism is the Disney Company and its suppliers for the amusement Park in Hong Kong. The conditions are comparable to the ones being reflected in the case before. The mainland factory workers are overworked, underpaid and exposed to filthy working conditions. Also the complete ranges of legitimate workers benefits are permanently ignored[253].

Moreover, official organizations are turning a blind eye on the current developments and working conditions. Until today, the IOC has refused to recognise minimum labour standards within the Olympic games-licensed companies. Although the discussed case was published the IOC still keeps a low profile and is not willing to take actions in order to encounter this situation. Although many supranational organizations addressed the IOC in order to demand for improvement of the prevalent working conditions[254].

But the Chinese work force is starting to react. Latest figures are showing that China's labour unrests are increasingly affecting the corporate world in China. The figures make a clear statement. Sources state that labour dispute cases skyrocketed from 19.000 reported cases in 1990 to 314.000 cases in 2005, involving 740.000 workers only in 2005[255]. Comparable figures are stated by an expert in this field, Ching Kwan Lee[256]. This development is remarkable in terms of business success in China. Chinese workers are increasingly aware of their basic rights and are gaining confidence in demanding their legitimate labour rights. This aspect has to be considered in future business activities undertaken by investors from abroad.

---

253 http://www.thestandard.com.hk/news_detail.asp?we_cat=4&art_id=53342&sid=15348812&con_type=1&d_str=20070913; See Arbeitsrecht31.pdf

254 http://www.playfair2008.org/index.php?option=com_content&task=view&id=71&Itemid=43; See Arbeitsrecht29.pdf; p. 2

255 http://www.worldpress.org/Asia/2925.cfm; See Arbeitsrecht16.pdf

256 cp. Against the Law; Ching Kwan Lee; p. 44

5. Labour Law in Taiwan

Taiwan is perceived to belong to mainland China by the central government. However, Taiwan is still keeping its sovereignty under any circumstances. Despite all the differences between Taipei and Beijing, the Labour Law system of both countries is comparable in many occasions.

5.1 Historical background

The legal system of Taiwan has been strongly influenced by continental Europe. The Japanese occupation and the republican system of the early 20th century also had remarkable ramifications on the development of the Taiwanese legal system. Particularly the German law system of the 1920s was used by the early Chinese Republic and thus transmitted to the island of Taiwan. As early as in the 1930s, the Chinese labour law was imposed to improve the situation of the workers[257].

The Taiwanese labour law originated form Continental China and was still valid until 1984. Many of the encoded regulations were transmitted into the new labour code form in 1984; the Labour Standard Law System (LSL)[258].The introduction of this legal system was strongly supported by the U.S. government at that period and has made a major contribution to its final implementation. Since 1998, every employment contract in the manufacturing sector has been governed by the LSL system[259] and is increasingly adopted by any sector of the Taiwanese economy.

5.2 Comparisons to continental china

Comparing the Chinese Labour Law System and the LSL, there are a few differences which have to be named. In regard to contracts of employment, the duration under LSL is categorically unlimited[260]. Taiwanese workers have to work 42 hours a week[261], although it is a

[257] See Arbeit in China; Rolf Geffken; p. 123
[258] See http://www.gti.com.tw/lawandregulations02.htm
[259] cp. Taiwanese Labour Standard Law; Art. 3
[260] See Arbeit in China; Rolf Geffken; p. 126
[261] cp. Taiwanese Labour Standard Law; Art. 30 sec. 1 Nr. 3

reduction from its former 48 hours, the legitimate working time in China lies below at 40 hours.

Another interesting fact is that the LSL system does not subdivide the statutory notice of termination into business-related, behaviour-based or individually related reasons. However, in practice most of the statutory notices of termination are based on a lack of operational performance of an enterprise, although high obstacles are placed for an employer, if he wants to terminate a contract of employment because of this reason[262].

One of the biggest differences with continental China is the Labour safety and health law, imposed in 1974 and amended in 1991, this law code provides a plethora of benefits for frontline workers and employees who have to work under dangerous conditions. Regular enterprises with more than 300 employees have to establish a medical health care centre within the company's compound. Firms that manufacture under dangerous conditions have to install such a centre starting with a workforce of 100[263]. Governmental labour law inspectors are appointed by the Taiwanese administration to monitor the compliance with the regulations.

Collective agreements only play a subordinate role in the working environment of Taiwan. One of the determinants displaying this fact is that these agreements usually only affect a certain company or enterprise, never a complete commercial sector[264]. Relevant collective agreements predominately exist in state-owned enterprises. Most of the private owned companies do not clinch any collective contracts. One of the core impediments is that any tariff autonomy is non-existent; a company has to show the tariff content to the official authorities. The tariff agreement is normally rejected, if the draft scales back the competitiveness of the respective enterprise. It is pretty obvious that this argument is widely used by the responsible labour bureau and does not create a favourable environment for the implementation of such a collective agreement[265]. Also company unions have to struggle with minor importance and a striking lack of influence. They are predominately

---

[262] See Arbeit in China; Rolf Geffken; p. 128

[263] ibid; p. 136

[264] ibid; p. 139

[265] ibid; p. 141

organised on a company level, but do not have any representative participation rights for their correspondent workforce[266].

5.3 Future perspective

The LSL has reached many achievements mainly concerning the individual labour law. In this area, the LSL hast the most profound impacts on the working society of Taiwan. The existing collective agreements are only few and far between, and do not provide working delegations with real bargaining power. Further more, the motherland is gaining influence on the Taiwanese political environment; it has already triggered profound implications concerning business issues. Many Taiwanese companies are changing their locations and are shifting to continental China. A severe exodus of capital is currently on its way. Some experts subscribe to the view that the LSL system might be channelled into the Chinese Labour Law system; however, this development is markedly questioned by a big majority of international law specialists. Taiwan will not only have to fight for its political independence, but also for its achieved labour law regulations[267].

[266] ibid; p. 143
[267] See Arbeit in China; Rolf Geffken; p. 151

6. Labour Law in Hong Kong

The situation in Hong Kong is significantly different compared to Taiwan in terms of relations to China mainland. The geographical scope and the reintegration to the PRC might have detrimental implications for the Hong Kong Law System in the long run.

6.1 Historical Background

Many law experts still postulate that the Hong Kong Law system is heavily influenced by the British, due to the colonial periods. The main difference is the social and political framework of the former British colony in which the Hong Kong Law Labour system is amended. Since the reintegration of this metro pole into China mainland, the central government is trying to limit the rights of the local administration in Hong Kong, with increasing success.

The Basic Law Code is the foundation of The Hong Kong Law system. It assures many rights that are comparable to Basic Laws of western societies'. For instance, the Basic Law provides the basic right of emigration[268], or the right to freely choose his attorney[269] or the right of academic freedom[270]. The most interesting regulation concerning the basic law is article eight, it safeguards that the complete plethora of regulations stays valid. And that all further regulations have to meet the standards of the Basic Law.

The Hong Kong Labour Law was not triggered by the British originally, but by the population of Hong Kong. During the Cultural Revolution in the 1960s, the citizens of Hong Kong demanded for stronger worker's rights to clearly separate them form the work force in China[271]. The result was the launch of the "Employment Ordinance", a law code that should assure basic rights to the workers in order to fight social desperation. In fact, one of the core impediments to introduce beneficial rights to the employees was the hierarchical structure of Hong Kong and the overwhelming power of the employers in this city. One of the major characteristics of the "Employment ordinance" is the basic right for the employers to

---

268 cp. Hong Kong Basic Law; Art. 31
269 cp. Hong Kong Basic Law; Art. 35
270 cp. Hong Kong Basic Law; Art. 34
271 See Arbeit in China; Rolf Geffken; p.166

establish labour regulations that are based on their beliefs and ideas. It is pretty obvious that an entrepreneur in Hong Kong focuses on the company's success rather than on the personal situation of his work staff. Most of the social reforms at that juncture governed health and social issues[272].

6.2 Current situation

In Hong Kong the Labour law is labelled by a minor protection character in aid of the employees. Hong Kong Employers capitalize on a high "flexibility" of the "Employment Ordinance".

This favourable situation for the company leaders impeded the development of collective agreements. Unions are non-existent or have only limited influence on enterprises' decisions.

Further more, the introductions of new regulations have to be transmitted to the Chinese central government. The central government has the right to approve the final regulations. In cases of conflict with basic beliefs or guidelines supported by Beijing, a ratification of the article is unlike.

Hong Kong is mainly a city of office employees. Only around 6.1 % of all workers are employed in the manufacturing sector and account for around 15.1 % of the gross domestic product[273]. The main amounts of businesses are situated in the service sector, particularly in the banking, real estates and insurance sector.

6.3 Future perspective

The development of the Labour Law in Hong Kong and the establishment of effective protection rights are closely linked to the policy making in China mainland. If Hog Kong is capable to preserve human rights its democratic structures within Hong Kong, than the Labour Law system in Hong Kong and its achievements might last over the next decades[274].

---

272 See Arbeit in China; Rolf Geffken; p. 168

273 http://www.auswaertiges-amt.de/diplo/de/Laenderinformationen/Hongkong/Wirtschaft.html; See Arbeitsrecht19.pdf; p. 1

274 See Arbeit in China; Rolf Geffken; p. 184

7. China's New Labour Contract Law

This section will deal with the latest developments in the Chinese Legal Developments, the draft of the New Chinese Labour Code and its core improvements and changes. We will elaborate on the several regulations and the effects for each actor that is affected by this new set of rules.

7.1 Development

China's draft of labour contract law stirred up a great deal of controversy among Chinese as well ass overseas legal experts. Experts from different nations including labour law experts from Germany[275] and the population itself were asked to contribute to the improvement of the Chinese Labour Contract Law. This development is unique in Chinese history; more than 190.000 citizens of the PRC handed in their proposals and displayed their point of view[276]. The first draft was presented in Beijing on March 20, 2006[277].

7.2 Controversial points of view and the altered regulations

However, foreign business people damned it as the return to the socialist "iron rice bowl"- system, a step back to planned economy - and threatened the Chinese government to withdraw investments from China. The law indeed strengthens the position of labourers, e.g., by making written contracts obligatory in all kinds of enterprises, discouraging short-term contracts, or expanding participatory rights of trade unions. It reflects the Chinese leadership's lasting and increasing fear of social unrest and future possible turmoils. The labour contract law complements the legal

---

275 http://www.fernuni-hagen.de/arbeitsrecht/aktuelles.shtml; See Arbeitsrecht32.pdf

276 http://www.amrc.org.hk/5903.htm; See Arbeitsrecht33.pdf ; p. 1

277 http://www2.china.ahk.de/download/news/isheet_Arbeitsvertragsgesetz.pdf; See Arbeitsrecht24.pdf; p. 1

framework of the emerging market economy in China; its full implementation will be a different matter[278].

Many Chinese Labour Law experts see in the new draft a regress of nearly 20 years. The formerly intended protection of migrant workers and employees from exploitation might lead to a planned economy from their point of view. But not only attorneys from overseas share this opinion, also consultants, members of human resource departments and members of chambers of foreign trade strongly oppose the new draft[279]. Also the Chamber of Commerce of the European Union cited that the new regulations might have downside effects on the growth of the Chinese economy. But there are European companies that refrained from this position[280]. Also politicians, including the president of the United States officially welcome the new draft, and strongly support its goals[281]. Also supranational organizations like the ITUC (International Trade Union Cooperation) regard this development as a serious chance to improve the workers situation and speak in favour of the new draft[282].

The paramount amount of criticism is concentrated on the following issues: limitations of contract of employment; probation time; compensation in case of dismissal and strengthen of union rights.

Written Form and limitation of contracts of employment

Contract clauses that are unclear and not specified have to be interpreted in favour of the employee (Art. 9/10 Labour Law of the PRC.) Limited contracts of employment become increasingly unattractive for employers. In case of expiration, the employer has to remunerate compensation to the employee (Art. 39 Labour Law of the PRC.) If the reasons for termination of contract are

278 http://www.giga-hamburg.de/index.php?file=cha_0604.html& folder= publikationen/archiv/ch_aktuell; See Arbeitsrecht23.pdf; p. 1

279 http://www.amcham-china.org.cn/amcham/home/index.php; See Arbeitsrecht18.pdf

280 http://www.laborstrategies.blogs.com/global_labor_strategies/files/ appendices_to_undue_influence.pdf; See Arbeitsrecht20.pdf; p. 6

281 ibid ; See Arbeitsrecht20.pdf; p. 10

282 www.ituccsi.org/IMG/pdf/ CHINA__ITUC_to_President_Hu_ Jintao_on_draft_contract_law_24_May_2007.pdf; See Arbeitsrecht22.pdf

illegitimate, the employer has to reemploy the worker if the employee wants to get his working position back. Whether the employer neglects to abide by the law, then he has to pay the double amount of the original compensation total (Art. 42 Labour Law of the PRC.)[283].

Timely limited contracts are only permitted to terminate in case of mass redundancies or serious infringements of enterprise rules. Also, insufficient work performance does not lead to a dismissal. (Art.31; 33/34 Labour Law of the PRC.).

If these protection clauses are going to be consequently enforced by the local authorities, the dedication of limited contracts of employment can entail a high degree of risks for the enterprises. So far, employers did not have to name any reasons for expiration of limited contracts. A further remarkable change is the fact that orally clinched employment contracts are instantly transformed into unlimited contracts of employment. The opposite is only effective if the employee does not agree with the transformation (Art. 9 Labour Law of the PRC).

Wang Zhaoguo, deputy chairman of the steady committee of the National People's Congress explained that these regulations are going to be fully implemented until end of 2008. Until end of next year, every company conducting business in China has the duty to clinch a formal written contract with his employees[284].

Hindered dismissals

The core objective of regulations governing dismissals is to alleviate the repercussions for the dismissed employees. The dismissal protection has been transferred to a wider group of persons. Mass redundancies have been hindered and probation times shortened. From originally six months, the probation period has been reduced to one month for workers in non-technological related positions, two months for employees in technology related positions. The complete period of six months continues to exist for highly skilled technological positions (Art. 13 Labour Law of the PRC).

283 http://www.giga-hamburg.de/index.php?file=cha_0604.html&folder=publikationen/archiv/ch_aktuell; See Arbeitsrecht23.pdf; p. 7

284 http://www.giga-hamburg.de/index.php?file=cha_0604.html&folder=publikationen/archiv/ch_aktuell; See Arbeitsrecht23.pdf; p. 8

If the employee decides to abandon his firm, he is not obliged to pay for his training, as long as the training period did not last longer than half a year (Art. 39, 42 Labour Law of the PRC)[285].

Limitation of temporary employment

There has been a rising of temporary employment within China. The New Labour Law also reacts on that issue. Temporary employment enterprises have to offer their employees standardised contracts of employment and beyond that, clinch contracts that clearly identify the activities of the worker. Without a clear determination of the activity pool, the borrowing company holds the responsibility for the employee. Furthermore, the borrowing time must not exceed the period of twelve months, otherwise, the indirect contract of employment turns into a direct employment of contract with the borrowing company. In case of non-realization of the contract of employment and the dismissal of the employee, the position can not be replaced by a further temporary worker[286].

More rights for Unions

Already in 2001, the trade union law has been altered and strengthened the position of the unions. Since 2001, company unions or local unions need to get informed in case of termination of a contract of employment. With the new regulations, the voice of the Unions are amplified, union deputies are irredeemable (Art. 7, 34 Labour Law of the PRC). Especially in situations in which more than 50 employees are going to be dismissed, negotiations have to be initiated with the union and they have to find a proper solution for both sides. Until that point, the employer had only the duty to supply information to the union in case of a forthcoming dismissal. Now they have to inform the deputies in advance in order to enable the union to take further actions and ask for objection (Art. 35, Labour Law of the PRC). Especially compendiums governing enterprise regulations need to be published in accordance with the union and specifically explained to the work force. If a compendium is not available, the union has the right to introduce regulations

285 ibid; See Arbeitsrecht23.pdf; p. 9
286 ibid; See Arbeitsrecht23.pdf; p. 9

governing the behaviour within the company. (Art. 5, 51 Labour Law of the PRC).

The core objective of this new set of rules is to compel foreign enterprises to install unions in their production facilities in China. Most of them have not established so far a union in their affiliates or joint-ventures. Another big issue is the impetus to protect the migrant workers, who are predominately employed on building sites. The central government wants to boost the member figures in unions from 13.8 percent up to 70 per cent[287].

7.3 Résumé and Expectations

The allegation that China would turn back into an "iron rice bowl" is completely over drafted. The extension of the labour law code is especially for European companies already well known and already applied in their home countries. And many of the points being discussed in the new draft are still moderate and lie below the standards of the multinational origin countries do many experts claim[288].

Nonetheless, certain points are highly opposed by companies' officials; especially the strengthening of the Unions is a controversial issue for many multinationals. Especially American-based co operations want to keep their sole sovereignty to dismiss employees[289].

The new regulations are in particular feared by Taiwanese of overseas Chinese conducted enterprises, which are well kwon for violating labour law issues in a constant manner.

The Central government in Beijing has a clear target. Social unrest and the risk of potential turmoils are rising from year to year. Beijing tries to establish a system that is ruled by the law, and not by the disposal of a few part of the population. Hu Jintao, chairman of the People's congress, stated that governments at all levels should do their best to safeguard people's legitimate rights and interests

---

287 http://www.giga-hamburg.de/index.php?file=cha_0604.html&folder=publikationen/archiv/ch_aktuell; See Arbeitsrecht23.pdf; p. 10

288 http://www.laborstrategies.blogs.com/global_labor_strategies/files/behind_the_great_wall_of_china.pdf; See Arbeitsrecht21.pdf; p. 5

289 ibid; See Arbeitsrecht21.pdf; p. 6

and to maintain social stability[290]. One of the instruments is the strengthening of the ACFTU's bargaining position in order to establish proper collective agreements[291].

Foreign companies have so far benefited from the flexibility on the Chinese labour market. Due to the new regulations, the human resource departments of the multinationals will have to change their employment policies. Limited and temporary contracts have become more unattractive for the employers in general, thus the cost for labour will probably increase. On the other hand, highly qualified employees are not capable to undertake the so-called "job hopping", a term used for employees that change frequently their position on high level of a companies hierarchy.

Taking the possible increasing labour costs, the chamber of commerce and industry of the European Union claimed that the labour costs might skyrocket to a level which enforces overseas companies to shift their operations to cheaper destinations.

However, the Chinese central government accepts this possible development. The Chinese administration is looking for a compromise in order to maintain economic and by the same token, try to upgrade the social security of its population.

Crucial is still the estimated level of enforcement. The amplified labour law code supplies the work force with a multitude of powerful tools. One of the great weak points was the powerless unions. The Communist is trying to support the establishment of unions that really are representing their employees without loosing their political influence on these organizations. This is definitely one of the big issues to solve. The Labour Code of 1994 was already pretty complete. However, the enforcement of the law was violated in particular by the overseas companies. There is no multinational providing a union in their operations within China. It is the same companies which are strongly demanding for more legal certainty[292]. Especially the intellectual property rights issue is heavily discussed among these enterprises. This leads to the

---

[290] http://www.giga-hamburg.de/index.php?file=cha_0604.html&folder=publikationen/archiv/ch_aktuell; See Arbeitsrecht23.pdf; p. 15

[291] http://www.chinadigitaltimes.net/tag/labor+law; See Arbeitsrecht30.pdf; p. 1

[292] http://www.giga-hamburg.de/index.php?file=cha_0604.html&folder=publikationen/archiv/ch_aktuell; See Arbeitsrecht23.pdf; p. 16

assumption that legal certainty should be enforced only on some certain fields. Legal certainty is demanded and welcomed as long as it does not affect the profit margin. And first steps are already initiated by FIEs in China, in order to minimize the amount of redundancy payments that will markedly increase with New Labour Code, are companies curtailing back their work staff at this juncture[293]. Experts claim that this development will even be enforced until the end of this year. Further reactions on the part of the multinationals will have to be awaited.

However, there is a high chance that the Chinese justice will select the fields of appliance of the new labour law regulations. James Zimmermann, the executive vice president of the American Chamber of Commerce mentioned[294], that implementation is always a wild card, and does strongly rely on the participants and its reciprocal obligations. It is hard to say, on which degree the situation for the work force in China will improve. Many of the powerful actors on the Chinese market suppose that the intentions of the Chinese Central will not have that profound repercussion on their operations in China.

---

293 http://www.china-labour.org.hk/public/contents/news?revision%5fid=50073&item%5fid=50072; See Arbeitsrecht14.pdf

294 http://www.giga-hamburg.de/index.php?file=cha_0604.html&folder=publikationen/archiv/ch_aktuell; See Arbeitsrecht23.pdf; p. 16

8. Chinese Labour Law and its implications on companies

In this paragraph this thesis will try to name the main factors that have to be considered by employees, native and from abroad and the overseas companies concerning their business operations in China by focusing on the prevalent legal labour terms.

8.1 Domestic Employees and the Chinese Labour Law

China is a huge country, and business success depends for instance heavily on the region in which operations are undertaken. The Contract Employment System was launched in the early 1980s in some experimental areas. However, many regions, particularly the municipalities of Shanghai, Shenzhen and Tianjin have implemented the new law only to a certain degree (compare section 3). One of the paramount reasons for overseas companies to choose China as a manufacturing destination is the cheap labour cost. In order to capitalize on this factor of production, companies that are investing in China have to be aware of a score of legal facts.

The Contract Employment system from 1995 was not specified enough to safeguard the employees. In addition to that, the existing rights were often violated and the workers heavily exploited by multinationals (compare chapter: cases).

The New Chinese Labour Law and its implementation deals with a score of points already displayed (compare section 7). However, the main objective of the Central government was to strengthen the position of Chinese workers. This aspect scared off many of the world leading companies and strongly opposed the introduction of the upgraded labour code, including some of the most popular and powerful companies of the globe. These enterprises claimed that the new regulations might have an adverse effect on the country's economy[295]. Furthermore, the companies gave proposals to alter certain sections or clauses, which they perceived to be incomplete and not detailed enough[296]. In this case, the American chamber of commerce and the multinationals being represented see the weakness point in the currently existing labour code. The institution

---

[295] http://www.amcham-china.org.cn/amcham/home/index.php; See Arbeitsrecht18.pdf; p. 2

[296] ibid; See Arbeitsrecht18.pdf; p. 8-26

pointed out that the main issue to be dealt with, is a prevailing and widespread lack of enforcement[297]. However, it is interesting to see, that many of the companies that signed this letter, were also inflicted in many cases, concerning labour law violation cases, mainly dealing with minimum wage infringements. The latest case that was published concerned the McDonalds Company. The fast food chain was not paying the minimum wage to their Chinese employees[298].

This incidents and further sources allege that foreign cooperation's want to maintain the current situation. An investing company in China, needs to be aware of the fact, that respective law can only be amended when a written contract of employment does exist, signed individually or collectively by workers and employers. Today, most of the Chinese employees do not have a valid written contract of employment.

There are ballpark figures quoting that 70% of all rural workers an 15 % of all urban workers are working under these circumstances[299].

The new set of rules will create an implied contract for any worker who receives a wage, providing the employees with basic rights and benefits[300]. This circumstance will boost the labour cost level, but by the same token, it will elevate the social freedom and commitment of the workers within the company. There are even experts that substantially support the introduction or implementation of a company union because they expect that the benefits of work force satisfaction will boost productivity over the long term[301].

China's competitive advantage relies on cheap labour. This major fact is endangered by tighter labour laws and an increased enforcement of this set of rules. This will probably boost the wage level and thus lead to improved living conditions for the Chinese working population and by the same token reduce the attractiveness of China as a low cost destination. At this juncture, companies still

---

[297] ibid; See Arbeitsrecht18.pdf; p. 30

[298] http://www.tagesspiegel.de/wirtschaft/Unternehmen-McDonald-s-China-Loehne;art129,2353066; See Arbeitsrecht34.pdf

[299] http://www.laborstrategies.blogs.com/global_labor_strategies/files/behind_the_great_wall_of_china.pdf; See Arbeitsrecht21.pdf; p. 4

[300] ibid; See Arbeitsrecht21.pdf; p. 5

[301] See Investment in China: A Question and Answer Guide on How to Do Business; Wang Yongjun; p. 97

have the possibility to benefit from the lax enforcement and the coherent low wages. However, if the Chinese working force improves its position, it will not only have a deep impact on domestic companies; more than that, it will probably affect further region outside the country[302].

Companies that want to offshore business to China should be aware of the following point. One of the main sources for high labour costs in Germany or Europe in general, is the strong influence of the unions and their bargaining power in their domestic markets. The organisational character of the European workforce is one of the major reasons, why western companies are struggling with their enterprises overall cost structure. The implementation of the new set of labour regulations will enable the Chinese employees to demand for more rights and benefits, an interaction between subordinates and executives and thus will lead to rising costs[303].

Lax labour law enforcement is still prevalent and is not likely to change over the short term. However, if a western company decides to set up production facilities in China in the near future some facts have to respected. For instance, the Contract Employment System allows FDI companies to hire locals only throughout local authorities. A pre-selection is often undertaken by theses authorities[304]. Foreign employers should also take into consideration that longstanding employment relationships and loyalty to a single enterprise are rather unusual in China. After clinching the written contract of employment, it has to be send over to local authorities for approval reasons[305].

8.2 Foreign Employees in China and the Chinese Labour Law

But only locals will not guarantee the affiliates success in China. In order to monitor the operations in China, western multinationals will have to dispatch own employees to their subsidiaries. Some

---

[302] http://www.laborstrategies.blogs.com/global_labor_strategies/files/behind_the_great_wall_of_china.pdf; See Arbeitsrecht21.pdf; p. 8

[303] ibid; p. 10

[304] http://www2.eycom.ch/china/services/legal/de.aspx; See Arbeitsrecht27.pdf; p. 3

[305] ibid; See Arbeitsrecht27.pdf; p. 4

Labour Law requirements that need to be observed are described in the following.

If the stay of the European employee exceeds more than one month than the responsible Western employer is obliged by law to provide a document, containing the subsequent data: the duration of the activity abroad; the currency in which the salary shall be paid; additional payments in connection with the assignment abroad and additional non-cash benefits, as well as conditions agreed upon for the return of the employee.

The composition of the employment contract of expatriates normally adheres to the duration of their stay. If the assignment in China is short, the European employment contract is often supplemented with a delegation agreement. If the assignment is a longer term, the European employment relationship is normally suspended and a temporary employment contract with the Chinese company is formally concluded. Finally, in the case of an undetermined assignment overseas, the European agreement is cancelled and local Chinese contract is clinched. In this case, the employee does not normally get a guaranteed right of return. It is possible that a local contract in China can be necessary because of regulations concerning the visa requirements.

However, practical experience displays a high complexity of the legal relationship. Therefore negotiations of an expatriate agreement should give reason to create a contractual basis that is concise and reflects the current situation. Important issues that need not be considered and listed; precise description of the position, the field of responsibility, if possible, the reporting line, regulations regarding salary and additional payments for the assignment abroad, regulations regarding currency alignment as well as a regulation of the tax liability in China and/or the home country. Special clauses have to be defined concerning the outward and return flight as well as any regular flights home, the rights and duties in case of transfer and the eventual return as well as the notice term and other questions that have to be arranged should be content of the employment relationship.

The principle of contract autonomy also applies in labour law. If not special law was agreed upon, the employment relationship is subject to the law of the country in which the services are provided, even if the employee is delegated to China. If the stay in China is not permanent and does not outstrip three years, the temporary character could be actually being regarded as preserved. As a consequence, from a legal point of view, the relevant European or Western Labour Law is applicable to the employment relationship with the home company.

Chinese Labour Law does not consider that contractual relation that the employee is working for a Chinese company in China. For this reason, a foreign employee would be subject to the Chinese Labour Law as a result of his/her actual occupation in China. However, it is not clear whether and to what extent employment contracts with foreign employees are actually governed by the Chinese Labour Law. Because of this uncertain legal situation, a choice of law and a place of arbitration outside China should be mutually agreed upon in writing, between the European and the Chinese partner company[306].

8.3 Ramifications on German and FDI enterprises

In recent sections of this thesis we have reflected the core points of the New Chinese Labour Law and the severe reactions that have been triggered through the ramification process. But how profound will be the actual impact on German companies and FDI companies in general?

Taylor Wessing, an international law firm with a high degree of reputation focussed on some certain points in one of the first studies available dealing with this issue. FDI co operations are usually implemented very fast and with a high degree of compliance to the literal wording of the Chinese Labour Code. This might be a downside compared to the position of local competitors which still can capitalize on some loopholes[307]. Advocators from Taylor Wessing advocate the position that the secondment related rules of the new Labour Contract Law also apply to secondments by FESCO or similar organizations of staff to a foreign resident representative

---

306 http://www2.eycom.ch/china/services/legal/de.aspx; See Arbeitsrecht27; p. 5-7

307 http://www.taylorwessing.com/website/generator/taylorwessing/pages/publications/brochuresAllStartPage,CmPart=com.taylorwessing.website,CmLocale=de,CmPage=72.2186.6762.html; cp. Arbeitsrecht28.pdf; p. 7

office. The proposed applicability to employment relationships for representative offices was dropped in the finally promulgated law.

Pursuant to article 26 a labour contract shall be invalid if the employer does coerce the employee with divergent content of the written contract of employment. It is strongly suggested that the contract of employment should be properly drafted and should entail several clauses in order to prevent invalidity of contract (Article 27)[308]. In former chapters we have laboured on the existence of a written contract. This fact is not only very important in terms ofvalidity of the employment relation. By non-existence, an employee is designated to demand twice the agreed salary (Article 82). Furthermore, if there is no written contract concluded after one year, the contract is deemed to be open-ended (Art.14). There is a specified exception; in case of part-time workers (less than 4 hours a day and less than 24 hours a week) oral contracts are permitted[309].

A well drafted written contract of employment will become more important for employers because ambiguous terms can not be interpreted anymore in favour of the employer. In case of disagreement, the clauses are replaced by collective contracts or State provisions. Experts claim that a professional Chinese translation has become essential and the Chinese wording is decisive. This circumstance can turn into a substantial competitive disadvantage to Chinese enterprises[310].

In addition to that, FDI companies can only agree on one single probation period that can not be extended (Art.19)[311]. A probation period is invalid when[312]:

(1) it exceeds the permitted length (Art. 83)

(2) if the labour contract only specifies the probation period (Art. 19)

---

308 ibid; cp. Arbeitsrecht28.pdf; p. 9

309 ibid; cp. Arbeitsrecht28.pdf; p. 10

310 ibid; cp. Arbeitsrecht28.pdf; p. 12

311 http://www.taylorwessing.com/website/generator/taylorwessing/pages/publicati-ons/brochuresAllStartPage,CmPart=com.taylorwessing.website,CmLocale=de,CmPage=72.2186.6762.html; cp. Arbeitsrecht28.pdf; p. 13

312 ibid; cp. Arbeitsrecht28.pdf; p. 14

(3) if the probation period is the same as the labour term (Art.19)

Employers need to be aware of the fact that the salary during the probation period should not be lower the lowest level for the same job with the employer or less than 80% of the salary afterwards. The minimum should be respected as well (Art. 20). If the probation period is exceed from the employer, than the employee is entitled to ask for compensation payments (Art. 83)[313].

Regarding non-competition clauses, the maximum duration has decreased from three down to two years. Enterprises from abroad are even more urged to protect their know-how and technologies. Moreover, does Article 24 form the Labour of China requests the parties to define the scope, territory and term of a non-competition clause, but does not link the validity of the Non-competition clauses to this[314]. The minimum compensation has also been significantly altered by the authorities. Formerly there was a minimum compensation of at least a year's salary; the promulgated law only requires compensation on a monthly basis (Art.23). Pursuant to Article 91 of the Labour Law of the PRC, the new employee is liable for evidenced losses with the employee for cases in which the new employer recruits an employee who has not yet terminated his employment with another company[315].

Taking a closer look on the type of contract of employment, the terms concerning the termination of contract of employment are identical between fixed and open-ended contracts. Severance is generally payed if a fixed term contract expires and is not renewed (Art. 46 (5), 44 (1)). FDI companies might establish extra budgeting for expenses concerning termination of fixed-term contracts. This point will probably encourage overseas co operations to conclude more unlimited contracts of employment. It is strongly suggested to sign open-ended term contracts where required by law. In case of violation, the employer has to pay 2 times the normal compensation rate (Art. 82 (2)). Severance payments are also foreseen if the employer proposes a termination and the parties have agreed on a

313 ibid; cp. Arbeitsrecht28.pdf; p. 15
314 ibid; cp. Arbeitsrecht28.pdf; p. 16
315 ibid; cp. Arbeitsrecht28.pdf; p. 17

termination agreement (Art. 46 (2)). Also in case of expiration of a fixed-term contract, unless the employee has rejected a prolongation despite being offered the same or better terms than those on the expiring contract (Art. 46 (5))[316]. The severance payments after termination depend on the length of employment. For each year worked a month salary is scheduled as compensation amount. For a period longer than six moths and less than one year, a month salary is effective. And half a month salary is scheduled for any period less than six months[317]. Overseas companies need to be aware of the fact, that there is no limitation on the severance amount except, the employee's month salary is more than three times the average monthly salary of the employer's location as officially published; the maximum severance pay is based on the cap amount. It may not exceed compensation for twelve working years (Art. 47 (2)). Termination against the law triggers a right of the employee to be reemployed or the employee is appointed to get further severance payments. But not more than twice the stipulated severance amount (Art. 87).

The New Chinese Labour does additionally amplify the liability for damages caused by company rule violating laws, a lack of the mandatory minimum content in labour contracts, in case of an invalid contract or when a termination certificate is not issued on time. Chinese authorities can impose penalties if an employee's ID card is kept by the authorities in violation of the law. Security deposits are collected from an employee; or salaries are not paid in time or below subsistence level. Also non-payment of severance payments leads to penalties.[318].

The discussed issues might have repercussions on the FDI enterprise policies in China. Attorneys worldwide advocate that the employers need to reconsider their current contract of employment drafts and might specify them more clearly. In particular clauses should be implemented into the contract of employment draft governing confidentiality issues. This topic is not only in terms of copyright

---

316 http://www.taylorwessing.com/website/generator/taylorwessing/pages/publicati-
ons/brochuresAllStartPage,CmPart=com.taylorwessing.website,CmLocale=de,CmPage=72.2186.6762.html; cp. Arbeitsrecht28.pdf; p. 21

317 ibid; cp. Arbeitsrecht28.pdf; p. 24

318 ibid; cp. Arbeitsrecht28.pdf; p. 27

infringement interesting in China but for the protection of trade secrets and the like. This position has already been backed up by experts since the emergence of the Contract employment system[319]. They also urge FIEs to prepare their corresponded HR departments with the upcoming of greater participation of the trade unions concerning HR issues[320].

---

319 See Der chinesische Arbeitsmarkt; Jutta Hebel publisher; Joachim Platter author; page 83

320 http://www.taylorwessing.com/website/generator/taylorwessing/pages/publications/brochuresAllStartPage,CmPart=com.taylorwessing.website,CmLocale=de,CmPage=72.2186.6762.html; cp. Arbeitsrecht28.pdf; p. 30

9. Conclusion

In recent years numerous treatises and collections of essays have been published in English about the Chinese legal system. Most give little, if any, attention to labour law. It is pretty difficult to get valuable information and evaluated data about the current situation in China and the legal framework.

Even those motivated that are interested in Chinese Labour Law; the task is beset with practical difficulties. In contrast to those employed in ministries of international trade and foreign affairs, labour administrators have had limited exposure to outside contacts and fewer opportunities for study and research abroad. Relatively few primary sources are available in English or German translation, and those translations are frequently of minor quality.

Main concern and particular on Chinese labour sources are evident. Issues dealing with constitutional law, intellectual property rights, environmental protection, bankruptcy, and securities regulation are more accessible and more frequently discussed among scholars.

However, due to this thesis and from a Western point of view, one can say that multinational companies originating from developed countries are inclined to view the populous nations of the developing world disparagingly, as boundless sources of cheap labour, skilled and unskilled. Such contempt carries over into a lack of interest in the real requirements of developing nations.

Because of the excellent risk management skills of both rural and urban populations, periods of economic hardship will not lead to widespread or prolonged social unrest some experts might claim. The rural population has flowed eastward in search of cash income. Among urban residents on spouse works a low-paying but secure state sector job while the other engages in potentially lucrative entrepreneurial activities. Indeed, the government's greatest challenge may be how to harness the enormous energy and resourcefulness of its people and the growing social unrest that is postulated by many other experts of the Chinese society and the inherent legal system.

Whatever economic or political benefits may be generated, reform does not come without social costs. Hardship is experienced by the lowest layers of the Chinese society which is still represented by the substantial majority of the Chinese population. The main victims of the fast growing Chinese economy are the weak, including women, children and the unskilled rural work force with little chances to get a good education. Nonetheless, the possibility remains that the worst abuses may be progressively eliminated through heightened rights consciousness, stricter law enforcement, collective organization, and the provision of legal aid.

The "rule of law" debate among Western scholars tends to draw absolute distinctions between an instrumental and moral view of law, which, in the case of China, is unnecessary and even harmful to the promotion of mutual understanding and cooperation. It is all too easily forgotten that society requires order for its very survival. The alternative is the law of the jungle, prevails in so many of the world's failed nation-states.

To be sure, China has a long road to travel towards equitable distribution of income, working conditions, and opportunities for advancement on the national level. At the same time, China possesses a rich repertoire of coping strategies. It is the oldest culture in the world that still exists and has always understood to round ship the main obstacles on their way to success.

Though not democratically elected, the current government does express the popular will that China should never again be occupied and exploited by foreign powers. And it is increasingly aware of the growing tension among their population and is starting to meet the basic requirements of their citizens. The New Chinese Labour Law and the fortification of the union in China might form the backbone of future improvements for the Chinese workforce. However, the next years will show, if the steps undertaken will satisfy the populations needs and by the same token, keep the outrageous speed of the economic growth. Once this is sure, China and its interactions with other countries and with international organizations, though modulated by compromise will finally be determined by its own interests.

IV. References

Literature

Berkowsky, Wilfried: Die personen- und verhaltensbedingte Kündigung, Unter Berücksichtigung des Betriebsverfassungsrechts und des Arbeitsgerichtsverfahrens, 4. Auflage, München, 2005

Diem, Andreas: Das Recht der Investitionen in China, 1. Auflage, Baden-Baden, 2000

Geffken, Rolf/Kei-Lin Ting: Arbeit in China, 1. Auflage, Baden-Baden, 2004

Hebel, Jutta/Schucher, Günter/Howell, Jude/Chan, Anita: Der chinesische Arbeitsmarkt, Strukturen Probleme Perspektiven, 1. Auflage, Hamburg, 2004

Josephs, Hillary K.: Labor Law in China, 2nd editon, Huntington, 2003

Kittner, Michael/Zwanziger, Bertram: Arbeitsrecht, Handbuch für die Praxis, 4. Auflage, Frankfurt, 2001

Krause, Rüdiger: Arbeitsrecht I, Individualarbeitsrecht, 1. Auflage, München, 2007-10-10

Lee; Ching Kwan: Against the Law, Labor Protests in China's Rustbelt and Sunbelt, 1st edition, Los Angeles, 2007

Wang, Yongjun: Investment in China, A Question and Answer Guide on How to Do Business, 1st edition, Los Angeles, 1997

Wörlen, Rainer/Kokemoor Axel: Arbeitsrecht, Lernbuch Strukturen Übersichten, 7. Auflage, Köln, 2005

Internet Sources

http://www2.eycom.ch/china/services/legal/de.aspx, Arbeitsrecht27.pdf

http://www.amcham-china.org.cn/amcham/home/index.php, Arbeitsrecht18.pdf

http://www.amrc.org.hk/5903.htm, Arbeitsrecht33.pdf

http://www.auswaertiges-amt.de/diplo/de/Laenderinformationen/Hongkong/Wirtschaft.html, Arbeitsrecht19.pdf

http://www.bda-online.de/www/bdaonline.nsf/id/AufgabenundZiele, Arbeitsrecht04.pdf

http://www.bdi.eu/de/bdi/72.htm, Arbeitsrecht03.pdf

http://www2.china.ahk.de/download/news/isheet_ Arbeitsvertragsgesetz.pdf, Arbeitsrecht24.pdf

http://www.chinadigitaltimes.net/tag/labor+law,Arbeitsrecht30.pdf

http://www.chinalaborwatch.com, Arbeitsrecht08.pdf

http://www.china-labour.org.hk/public/contents/news?revision%5fid=50073&item%5fid=50072, Arbeitsrecht14.pdf

http://www.chinapolitik.de/studien/china_analysis/no_45.pdf, Arbeitsrecht09.pdf

http://www.dgb.de/mitglied_werden/index_html, Arbeitsrecht06.pdf

http://www.dgb.de/mitglied_werden/index_html, Arbeitsrecht06.pdf

http://www.export.gov/china/shanghaicontacts.asp, Arbeitsrecht13.pdf

http://www.fernuni-hagen.de/arbeitsrecht/aktuelles.shtml, Arbeitsrecht32.pdf

http://www.giga-hamburg.de/index.php?file=cha_0604.html&folder=publikationen/archiv/ch_aktuell, Arbeitsrecht23.pdf

http://www.gov.cn/english/2005-10/02/content_74185.htm, Arbeitsrecht17.pdf

http://www.info-arbeitsrecht.de/Kuendigungsschutz/kuendigungsschutz.html, Arbeitsrecht02.pdf

http://www.ituccsi.org/IMG/pdf/CHINA__ITUC_to_President_Hu_Jintao_on_draft_contract_law_24_May_2007.pdf, Arbeitsrecht22.pdf

http://www.laborstrategies.blogs.com/global_labor_strategies/files/appendices_to_undue_influence.pdf, Arbeitsrecht20.pdf

http://www.laborstrategies.blogs.com/global_labor_strategies/files/behind_the_great_wall_of_china.pdf, Arbeitsrecht21.pdf

http://www.manager-magazin.de/koepfe/artikel/0,2828,446123,00.html, Arbeitsrecht05.pdf

http://www.newsgd.com/news/guangdong1/200608310078.htm; Arbeitsrecht15.pdf

http://www.nyulawglobal.org/globalex/China.htm, Arbeitsrecht01.pdf

http://www.playfair2008.org/docs/playfair_2008-report.pdf, Arbeitsrecht10.pdf

http://www.playfair2008.org/index.php?option=com_content&task=view&id=71&Itemid=43, Arbeitsrecht29.pdf

http://resources.alibaba.com/article/2492/Concepts_in_Chinese_culture.htm; Arbeitsrecht11.pdf

http://www.taylorwessing.com/website/generator/taylorwessing/pages/publications/brochuresAllStartPage,CmPart=com.taylorwessing.website,CmLocale=de,CmPage=72.2186.6762.html, Arbeitsrecht28.pdf

http://www.tagesspiegel.de/wirtschaft/Unternehmen-McDonald-s-China-Loehne;art129,2353066, Arbeitsrecht34.pdf http://www.tdctrade.com/econforum/boc/boc030101.htm, Arbeitsrecht07.pdf

http://www.thestandard.com.hk/news_detail.asp?we_cat=4&art_id=53342&sid=15348812&con_type=1&d_str=20070913, Arbeitsrecht31.pdf

http://www.weltderarbeit.de/bericht2.htm, Arbeitsrecht25.pdf

http://www.worldpress.org/Asia/2925.cfm, Arbeitsrecht16.pdf

http://www.woek-web.de/.../publikationen/heuer_2004_vr_china_das_novellierte_gewerkschaftsgesetz.pdf, Arbeitsrecht26.pdf

Law Sources

Bürgerliches Gesetzbuch (BGB) in der Fassung vom 1. März 2005, S. 698

Grundgesetz (GG) der Bundesrepublik Deutschland vom 1. März 2007, S. 605

Tarifvertragsgesetz (TVG) in der Fassung vom 1. März 1997, S. 470

Constitution of the People's Republic of China, Arbeitsrecht12.pdf

Labour Law of The People's Republic of China; Arbeitsrecht35.pdf and Arbeitsrecht36.pdf